1D

THE
ONE DIRECTION
STORY

DANNY WHITE

MICHAEL O'MARA BOOKS

This paperback edition first published in 2013
First published in hardback in Great Britain in 2012 by
Michael O'Mara Books Limited
9 Lion Yard
Tremadoc Road
London SW4 7NQ

A CIP catalogue record for this book is available from the British Library.

Papers used by Michael O'Mara Books Limited are natural, recyclable
products made from wood grown in sustainable forests. The
manufacturing processes conform to the environmental regulations of the
country of origin.

ISBN: 978-1-78243-013-1 in mass market paperback print format
ISBN: 978-1-84317-968-9 in hardback print format
ISBN: 978-1-84317-990-0 in trade paperback print format
ISBN: 978-1-84317-973-3 in EPub format
ISBN: 978-1-84317-974-0 in Mobipocket format

1 2 3 4 5 6 7 8 9 10

Designed and typeset by Design 23, London
Printed and bound by CPI Group (UK) Ltd, Croydon, CR0 4YY

www.mombooks.com

CONTENTS

INTRODUCTION

A month can be a long and eventful time in pop music – just ask One Direction. For instance, for Liam, Louis, Niall, Harry and Zayn, the thirty days of April 2012 were packed with international incident and intrigue, terrific triumphs and torturous torment. Just two years previously they had been five ordinary teenage boys, counting the days before they auditioned as solo hopefuls on *The X Factor*. Their lives have been anything but ordinary ever since.

During April they were invited to the White House by Michelle Obama. They announced – and then sold out in record time – a headline concert at America's most prestigious concert venue, Madison Square Garden. They entered the studio to record with the Canadian king of pop, Justin Bieber. As the United States fell in love with the band, they appeared on the top American entertainment television programmes *The Today Show* and *Saturday Night Live*. Meanwhile, a shadow was cast over their American dream as they faced a lawsuit from a US band of the same name. Members of the American band soon received death threats from furious fans of their British namesakes.

As April continued, the band jetted to the southern hemisphere. There, they were delighted to discover that Australian and New Zealander girls are just as devoted to them as their American and British counterparts. The band was mobbed by an army of fans in Sydney and, on one occasion, a young man with no connection to the band was even surrounded by screaming fans in a moment of mistaken identity. As security tightened, one Australian fan said she would be willing to risk being shot to get close to them. Then, a slice of toast, half-eaten by band member Niall, went to auction. It attracted bids of nearly £100,000.

While celebrating the news that their debut single had passed the one million copies sold milestone in America, each band member pocketed a reported £2 million. Louis decided that he quite fancied buying a pet monkey. As if all this was not enough for one month, they were simultaneously flattered and deflated when they were praised by pop princess Rihanna and then told that Madonna had announced that she does not know who they are. Before the month was over the band also kissed some koalas, prompting fears that they had caught chlamydia from the bears that had urinated on them, and then they went surfing in the Pacific Ocean. There was still time for Niall to contract food poisoning and for two other members to take part in a 192-metre bungee jump. Then they arrived back in Britain, greeted, as ever, by thousands of screaming fans.

No wonder the frenzy that surrounds One Direction has been compared to 'Beatlemania': their popularity is simply immense however you measure it. They are the first UK pop group to debut at number one on the American album chart. The same album went straight to number one in Britain and twelve other countries. They have over 12 million followers on Twitter and 3.6 million on Facebook. They have amassed over 204 million YouTube views. A Google spokesperson has revealed that 3.35 million people are typing One Direction related phrases into the search engine each month.

One Direction are Britain's – and arguably the world's – biggest boy band. How they became so is a fascinating and inspiring story.

1 HARRY STYLES

When the five members of One Direction finally get a chance to stop working for a moment, take a proper breather and begin to survey the success they have made of their pop careers to date, none will be as calm and unruffled about it as Harry Styles. Harry's loveably nonchalant persona is not some contrived attempt at achieving an image of 'pop cool'; he really is, at heart, a laidback chap. His detachment has been tested, too: life had bowled him some cruel balls in the years before he became famous but he played them all with a cool, straight bat, rarely breaking sweat for long.

As for Harry's mum, Anne Cox, when she stops and thinks about the fame her son has acquired and his many professional achievements, she finds it harder to get her head around it. To the outside world, he might well be the pin-up singer from One Direction, a young man known in many countries and endlessly discussed by both his fans and the mainstream media. To Anne, he will always be something else as well: 'At the end of the day, he's my little baby and there he is on stage in front of millions of people,' she said.

Anne's little baby was born on 1 February 1994. He was her second child – she already had a young daughter called Gemma. Anne was just as thrilled when she became a mother second time around. She named her precious baby son Harry Edward. No one knew it then, but a star had just been born.

His early years were spent in Cheshire, in the north west of England. It is an area of lush rural beauty surrounding a number of built-up towns and villages. Holmes Chapel, one of those villages, is where Harry spent much of his childhood. It is a comfortable neighbourhood with most basic amenities, including easy public transport for those who want to hit the big smoke of Manchester for something wilder. Cheshire itself is not an area with a massively famous artistic heritage, though rock singers of yesteryear Ian Curtis and Tim Burgess both come from there. When he auditioned for *The X Factor*, Harry described the area as 'quite boring – nothing much happens there', though on a more admiring note he admitted, with a cheeky smile, that it is 'picturesque'. He is now one of Cheshire's most famous sons.

As the baby Harry became a toddler, he was sent to a nursery called Happy Days. Harry feels it is an appropriately named institution as he had so many enjoyable times there. It was a small establishment so he was never short of attention and care. During his nursery years he was a well-behaved boy and concentrated on playing with toys and participating in games. He has always been a fun-loving chap. A creative one, too: he began to show his artistic side at home at the breakfast table, where he would draw on his toast with food colouring before he ate it. He was always encouraged to express himself, a key factor in the development of any budding artist. In time he learned to juggle and tried his hand at learning some musical instruments. Always funny and entertaining, he was becoming something of an all-rounder. 'He's always loved attention and making people laugh,' Anne told *NOW* magazine. 'He's certainly not shy about himself. Ever since he was young he's made people smile. I always thought he'd end up on the stage.'

When he was seven, Harry's life, which had been generally very happy and enjoyable until then, took a darker turn when his parents told him that they were going to get divorced. His first reaction to this bombshell was to burst into tears. He loves both his parents, so hated to think of them going their separate ways. At seven years of age Harry would most likely to have been in a double-bind: old enough to understand the pain caused by the separation but not yet old enough to understand or control his own reaction to the pain. Children of that age who face such a testing upheaval typically go through feelings of grief, shame, resentment, confusion and even anger as they come to terms with the situation.

Though Harry has always put an upbeat spin on his reaction to the divorce in public, it will have hurt him and – to some extent – influenced the course of his life since the split. He says he bounced back fairly quickly and learned to live with the situation. As he has confirmed since, as a seven-year-old he did not – and *could* not – fully grasp what was going on in his parents' minds. There were many practical changes for him to come to terms with. After the divorce he and his sister moved house with Anne, settling in a more rural part of Cheshire and living above a pub where Anne became the landlady. There were lots of changes going on in his life but Harry managed to roll with the punches. He made a new friend, a boy called Reg who was a little older than him, and got to know the new area. One of the hangouts he took delight in discovering was a dairy farm where they made delicious ice cream a few miles from his new house. He loved the ice cream there, and life always felt good when he tucked into one after cycling down the road.

Despite his parents' divorce, Harry remained full of energy and enthusiasm. Rather than ever truly misbehaving – he only got into one fight throughout his school years – he channelled his drive into hard work. He particularly enjoyed English and RE classes. In English he found he was good at expressing himself on the page and often achieved good grades for his essays. An extrovert at heart, he also looked forward to drama classes, and it was through these that he made his debut public singing appearance. 'The first time I sang properly was in a school production – the rush that I got was something that I really enjoyed and wanted to do more of,' he said. That rush was the feeling of his love of performing and being in the spotlight being satisfied. The plays that Harry appeared in included *Chitty Chitty Bang Bang*, in which Harry played the part of Buzz Lightyear. Although that character, originally from the *Toy Story* franchise, is not a traditional part of the *Chitty Chitty Bang Bang* story, this being a school production some liberties had been taken with tradition. As an Aquarian by star sign, Harry has always been comfortable with experimentation so that was fine by him. On another occasion he played the title role in a play about a mouse called Barney.

However, acting was just one part of Harry's performing ways – he was soon also being encouraged to sing. It was his father who first sparked his interest in music. As it became clear that Harry loved to sing, his grandfather bought him a karaoke machine and one of the first songs that Harry crooned along to on it was Elvis Presley's 'Girl of My Best Friend'.

It was when he was at the Holmes Chapel Comprehensive School on Selkirk Drive that Harry stumbled upon an exciting way of further fulfilling his desire to perform in front of an audience, when he was invited to join a rock band. A friend of his, named Will, was looking for a lead vocalist for a band he was assembling. He asked Harry to come along and practise with the band. All the members were very happy with handsome Harry as their front man and the band's line-up was complete.

Then they just needed to agree on a name for themselves. It was Harry who suggested the random name White Eskimo. It is a rather strange moniker – sounding more like a nightclub or a cocktail than a teenage rock band. Nevertheless, it was certainly distinctive and nobody had any better ideas, so they went with it. Harry has an inventive mind: this would not be the last time that he came up with a band name. White Eskimo was influenced by punk-pop acts such as Californian band Blink-182. Harry is also a fan of Jack's Mannequin and other related artists. However, three of his biggest musical inspirations stood entirely outside the punk-pop genre during their iconic careers: Michael Jackson, Elvis Presley and Freddie Mercury. Other songs he loved during his childhood include 'Free Fallin'' by John Mayer and he also had a soft spot for the material of Michael Bublé. Each member of White Eskimo had their own influences – and together they made for a fairly decent musical outfit.

Soon, they played at school events – and at a wedding. The first song that White Eskimo ever performed live together was Bryan Adams's 'Summer of '69'. Then, the band noticed there was a local talent show being held for groups. They decided to enter it, as Harry later explained to *X Factor* host Dermot O'Leary on the programme. 'We entered a "Battle of the Bands" competition about a year and a half ago and we won. Winning Battle of the Bands and playing in front of that many people really showed me that's what I wanted to do. I got such a thrill when I was in front of people singing, it made me want to do more and more.'

The victory had also made an impression on Harry's headteacher Denis Oliver, who was present at the competition, held in the school canteen. Mr Oliver remembered later: 'White Eskimo won the Battle of the Bands here when he was in Year 10. He's performed in a lot of assemblies.' Harry's singing had clearly made quite an impact on those who formed his first live audiences.

Indeed, some of the children who were at those shows have since remembered what they saw. Bethany Lysycia, for instance, told the *Crewe Chronicle*: 'They were really good. Everyone was really impressed, especially with Harry. We all knew he could sing because we would see him singing in the corridors all the time. He was always going to be a star and I think he's getting better and better.'

Videos have been published on the internet of the band performing 'Summer of '69' at a wedding. Although Harry's voice is, naturally, quite a lot higher in these videos than it is now, he cuts a familiar figure on the stage: he bounces, looks down at the floor as he takes deep breaths, and generally comes across as the same lad who is now in One Direction. Another song that they played regularly was by the band Jet, and was called 'Be My Girl'. In another video the band is seen rehearsing. Their sense of fun is clear.

Their wedding performance earned them their first pay packet: the band was paid £160 for the show. They split it evenly between them meaning each got £40. As Harry remembered fondly, they were also offered free sandwiches. However, more valuable than the money and sandwiches combined was the experience and the feedback. People were telling him that he was a natural singer and front man. His charisma and stage presence were such that one guest at the wedding, a music producer and therefore a man with expert eyes, compared him with one of British music history's finest front men, Mick Jagger of The Rolling Stones. What an honour: Harry felt so proud and excited by all the positive feedback he received. He was becoming a mini local celebrity and pin-up long before he became nationally and then internationally famous. That fact, together with his boyish good looks and charming ways, meant he was getting plenty of attention from girls long before he shot to national fame through *The X Factor*.

He rates a friend he had at the age of six as his first close female friend. She was the daughter of a friend of Anne's and the two were very sweet together. Harry even bought them matching teddy bears. He describes her as 'the cutest little girl'. At the age of twelve he got his first proper girlfriend and he has stated that his 'first snog' was with a girl from his school.

A girl called Lydia Cole told the *Crewe Chronicle* that Harry had been her first boyfriend, while they were both at school. 'What you see on screen is what you get,' she said. 'That's Harry – he's always been charming and cheeky'. Rumours that circulated about Harry once he became famous through One Direction portray him as very experienced with girls and very quick to show off about his prowess. 'Harry was bragging about how many girls he'd slept with', an 'insider' quoted by *Now* magazine claimed. 'The number he said was six'. They added: 'Harry's very flirty'. Of all the members of 1D, it was Harry who seemed most assured when dealing with attractive female personalities during their time on *The X Factor* and beyond.

The legacy of his past experience was visible in the smooth, confident and assured persona he took when speaking with them and belied his tender years.

As for his family, it got a new member when his mother met his stepdad, Robin. The couple had been careful to consider Harry and Gemma's feelings by introducing their partnership gradually and sensitively. Harry thought Robin was great and was delighted – if a bit amused – to learn that he had proposed to Anne while they sat watching the soap opera *Coronation Street*.

Other memories from his childhood include the time he ate way too much food at a TGI Fridays restaurant and vomited over his sister Gemma on the way home. His love of food never caused weight issues for Harry, partly because he loves sport, with badminton, football and cricket being three of the games that he enjoyed taking part in. He also became a feared opponent at the bowling alley. Unsurprisingly, one of his favourite classes at school was PE. He began to represent the local football team, often playing in goal.

He got himself a part-time job working at a local business, the W. Mandeville Bakery. His boss, Simon Wakefield, told the BBC that Harry had been a model employee. 'He used to clean the floor at night and work on a Saturday, serving customers in the shop. He was great, he was good to have around – there was always a good atmosphere when he was about.' Harry's former boss also said the youngster 'was really popular with the customers when he used to work on counter'. One can imagine his charisma and good looks going down a treat.

Harry was ready to transfer his natural charm onto the national stage. Like millions of other Britons, he loved to watch television talent shows, including *The X Factor*. When he saw young contestants, in particular, succeed on that series, he began to believe that he too stood a chance of doing so. To use a phrase that would become apposite for him in the future, he dared to dream. Local talent shows and weddings were all very well, but to audition in front of the fearsomely respected Simon Cowell and his fellow judges, as well as millions of television viewers, was an entirely different prospect. So he grabbed an application form, which Anne filled in for him, and then posted off. From then, it was just a case of counting down the days to his audition. He told his bandmates what he planned to do and they had no hard feelings. The bass guitarist Nick Clough said: 'We're happy for him and wish him all the best'. The lead guitarist, Haydn Morris, said: 'Everyone here at school is behind him. It's great.'

Although fired with ambition and hope, Harry was actually open-minded about his life plans in the years ahead as he approached his *X Factor* audition. All he knew was that whatever he ended up doing as a job, he would want it to be something he could earn a good living from. He did not want to struggle financially as an adult. He had plans to go to college and study Law, Business and Sociology at A Level. In his spare time he worked at the bakery. As we shall see, some of the other boys who ended up in One Direction arrived to audition very much on edge emotionally. They felt their very future was hanging on getting a 'yes' from the judges. Blasé Harry was keen to succeed but was less uptight about the outcome. For him, the experience was more one of discovery: he wanted to know whether he had it in him to become a professional singer. If the answer turned out to be negative, that was fine by him, but at the very least he'd give it a shot.

Sometimes, when someone has a dream in life, they find a reason not to pursue it. Rather than focusing on all the things that could go right, they imagine things that could go wrong. Harry's example shows that at times it is worth taking the more simple and positive approach of simply pausing to consider whether one has anything to lose by giving it a go. He did not approach *The X Factor* with a fear that his life depended on success. He just decided to try it out and see what happened. Life is full of choices – young Harry Styles had just made a very wise one.

2 LOUIS TOMLINSON

Louis is something of the dark horse of the band. Unlike Harry, Liam and Niall, and even Zayn to an extent, he was basically absent from our screens as the early phases of *The X Factor* were broadcast. Few viewers had noticed him much prior to the judges' houses phase. Even once the band was assembled and thrust into the live shows, Louis was one of its less prominently featured members. In the aftermath of the series, as One Direction took the first steps in their career, his very inclusion in the band was called into question by an embittered former winner of the popular talent show. Many would have been disheartened to have such a lesser stature. Not Louis – he kept his head up, continued to pull that winning smile of his, and before long he was a firm favourite with the fans, sometimes receiving the loudest cheers and screams of all the members during concerts and public appearances.

It took some poise and assurance to manage that. As the eldest child in his family, Louis has rarely lacked for either. He has four younger sisters, Phoebe, Daisy, Félicité and Charlotte. As a first-born child he is expected to have certain inherent characteristics, among which are a strong sense of duty and responsibility and an ability to lead. This is largely because the eldest child in a family, particularly a large clan like the Tomlinsons, usually has an almost semi-parental role in the home. They are good at nurturing and caring for others. Louis has stated that people have sometimes been impressed by how well he deals with children. 'First borns' can also, on a less positive note, be prone to self-criticism, and feelings of envy and guilt. Behind his carefree image, Louis has moments of unhappiness and uncertainty.

In truth, though, the fact he is the only boy in the family had as much of an affect on his life as his place in the birth order. It made him very close to his mother from the early days.

That fond relationship endures to this day, even as he is frequently thousands of miles from her. The Tweets between mother and son on Twitter alone testify to their closeness. So do their pronouncements. 'We've got a close relationship,' said Johanna. 'He's got four sisters and he is my only boy. He is a lovely family lad.' With such a large age gap between him and his youngest sisters – the twins Daisy and Phoebe – he was often asked to muck in with some of the duties around the home, which he did, happily and effectively. Childhood photos of Louis often show him caring for his sisters. In one famous image, his sister Charlotte is sitting on his lap as he reads a book to her. He loves all his sisters. That does not preclude him wishing he could have had a brother as well. In the absence of one, he and his dad formed a close bond as the only males in the crowded Tomlinson household.

As all of the band's fans are only too aware, Louis is comfortably the chattiest member of One Direction. His love of speaking, speaking and then speaking a bit more actually long predated the band. Even when he was still in a pram, Louis would be talking for most of the day. Strangers on the street would find themselves greeted out loud by the cute-faced kid in the pram. If they did not respond with sufficient friendliness they could find themselves the subject of a less affable, follow-up comment from loquacious Louis. He was full of so much energy and character – there seemed to be something special about Johanna's 'lovely family lad' from the start.

He was a lovely family lad who was prone to dreaming as a child. Before he settled on singing as a career, Louis dreamt of being, among other things, a Power Ranger, a footballer, a farmer, a drama teacher and an actor. It is pertinent that Louis was so crazy about the Power Rangers. He admits that as a child he became 'obsessed' with them and for several Christmases running he would ask for a Power Rangers toy or some other sort of merchandise. When the family moved for a while to Poole, near Bournemouth, he was thrilled to learn that there were Power Ranger rides on the seafront. His future bandmate Zayn Malik was, unbeknown to Louis at this stage, also a Power Rangers obsessive. A more intriguing coincidence comes in the fact that the man who would later make the boys' dreams come true had played a significant part in the Power Rangers story. Simon Cowell, noting the huge viewing figures the series was attracting on television, signed a deal to release Power Rangers songs. One of these releases reached number three in the charts. In years to come, Cowell would put Louis at the top of the charts.

First, though, Louis had various stages to go through as he developed his love of entertainment. Indeed, his early love of performance was of the acting rather than singing variety. He was soon taking small parts as an extra on television shows. This run began when he blagged his way onto the cast of a show in which his twin sisters were appearing. At one show he participated in he met the celebrity James Corden off set and they remain friends to this day. He took acting classes and was even ambitious enough to make an arrangement with a theatrical agent. Parts – albeit small ones – followed, including one in the long-running BBC show *Waterloo Road* and another in an ITV drama called *If I Had You*. He also acted at school and one of the highlights of his pre-*X Factor* life was when he secured the lead role of Danny in a production of *Grease*.

He almost burst with pride and excitement at this achievement. There were 200 people in the audience and it is reported that he made for a reasonably compelling leading man.

Away from acting, Louis always made an impact at school. Later, he was remembered vividly – if sometimes with contradictions – by several of the staff who taught him. His headteacher, Yvonne Buckley, made a nod to his fine elder sibling role when she said: 'Louis was a hardworking and determined pupil who is extremely supportive of his sisters.' Buckley's memory of Louis as 'hardworking' is challenged by his former head of year, Jenni Lambert. 'I'm absolutely delighted for him,' she told the *Daily Star*. 'He was a bit of a rogue at school at times, but he absolutely loved performing, and the thing he lived for most was performing with the band at assemblies. Performing was what he always wanted. He is a very charming chap, but he wasn't a great fan of doing academic work.' That said, she concludes that: 'He has a very likeable quality.' He has provided her with a shining example to use to motivate her pupils. If they work hard, she tells them, they too could go on to become as successful as Louis has.

Despite his early acting success – a discipline to which Louis aspires to return one day in the future – it was music that made him the example that Lambert can now use. When he was fourteen he joined a band called The Rogue. He is proud to have been in the band and is very proud of their name (it is certainly more evocative of a rock band than Harry's White Eskimo). The story of how he came to join is an unconventional one. The other members of the band became friendly with Louis during a school trip to Norfolk and they asked him if he would like to be their lead singer. It says much about Louis's inherent star quality that they asked him this without even knowing whether he could sing or not. If one were to look for ways of demonstrating that a person has that indefinable yet important quality that is known as 'the x factor' here is such a moment. Louis's charismatic personality – plus, perhaps, his cute face – had been enough to convince an already-formed band that he was the man to lead them from the front.

Fortunately, once he did sing for them they

were happy with what they heard. The Rogue was now complete. Their sound was more 'rocky' than that of One Direction. Among the acts whose songs they attempted were American punk-pop stadium band Green Day, who are best known for their anthems 'American Idiot', 'Wake Me Up When September Ends' and 'Good Riddance (Time of Your Life)'. As we have seen, Harry, too, was a fan of their lively, romping sound. The Rogue also tried out songs by another American rock outfit: The Killers. When Louis sang these bands' songs he partly imagined himself as their respective lead singers – Billie Joe Armstrong and Brandon Flowers – but also paid attention to bring himself into the performance.

In time he would be a real star, with all the trappings that come with that – including girls. His first kiss came in Year Five. 'I don't really remember that much about it,' he told the website Sugarscape. 'It was one of those kind of like ... kind of weird moments. It was all right. I was young, I was naive. What can I say?' The following year he got his first celebrity crush – on the *Harry Potter* actress Emma Watson. He remembers falling for her charms when he and his classmates went to watch the first *Harry Potter* movie. 'Literally all the lads fancied [her],' he said.

As he entered his teenage years Louis started dating a girl who he 'really liked'. However, a few weeks later she ended their relationship because, she told him, he 'wasn't good looking enough'. Recounting the story after becoming a pin-up through One Direction, Louis's pain was still palpable. 'It still hurts me inside', he said. His fans nowadays are flummoxed that any girl dared dump their hero.

Even taking into account that Louis is the oldest member of One Direction, his childhood was still a busier and more eventful experience than his bandmates'. He was an energetic boy in a hurry, keen to try as many of the things that life offered as possible. His curriculum vitae is packed with the many jobs he tried. As a teenager Louis worked as a football coach, selling snacks at a football stadium, as a waiter, at a branch of the well-known chain Toys R Us and at a cinema.

Soon, though, it became time for him to apply

to audition for *The X Factor*. He applied in 2009 but did not make it past the very first round. He spent the next year determined to return and to make more of a success of it. When he reapplied for the 2010 series he had just finished his AS Levels. His life would never be the same again.

3 ZAYN MALIK

Given his almost idyllically handsome features, including his magnificent mane of dark hair, Zayn could have taken a different career path to the one he has. He could easily have gone on to be a model, for instance. It would have been even easier for him to become a bit of an arrogant bore – plenty of good-looking young celebrities are. They quickly realize that their fine features are enough to open doors for them and decide they therefore have no need to exude any genuine charm. As for Zayn, despite his undeniable slice of vanity, he has avoided these pitfalls and has instead remained the kind, down-to-earth and slightly eccentric character he always has been.

Zayn Malik – his name is also sometimes spelt 'Zain' – was born on 12 January 1993. His mum is called Tricia, and his dad's name is Yaser. He comes from a large and friendly family: Zayn has three sisters, five aunties, two uncles and over twenty cousins. Having so many female relatives, as his bandmate Louis does, has made Zayn particularly empathetic to women. Not only that: Zayn is the second oldest sibling in his immediate family, and 'middle born' children are believed to have particularly strong powers of empathy and sensitivity to the needs of others. His middle born status also means that Zayn is more inclined to fight on behalf of the weak or the underdog. All of these exciting facts – taken together with his good looks and success – make him rather fine boyfriend material.

But what sort of boy was he and what kind of childhood did he have? His earliest memory was of a trip to the fairground with his mother and grandmother. For the three-year-old Zayn this was quite an experience. All the lights, noise and general sense of excitement left a big impression on the toddler. Although Zayn loved being the centre of attention at home, on this outing his attention and all his senses were captivated by what was going on around him. As a celebrity his life is colourful, hectic and exhilarating most of the time now – a bit like a non-stop fairground, one could say.

He attended Lower Fields primary school, on Fenby Avenue in Bradford. The school's motto is 'Sharing the Vision, Achieving Success'. While he was there he began to develop the passion that would eventually jettison him to global celebrity. 'I've always loved singing,' he said. During his primary school years Zayn gave one of his first public performances when he sang as part of a choir for the Lord Mayor at a Bradford branch of the Asda supermarket chain. He also took part in theatrical pursuits. The headteacher of Lower Fields, John Edwards, said of his now famous former pupil: 'I remember he was a nice young man, hard-working and I remember in particular his leading role in the Year Six leavers' play.'

There were indeed many happy times for Zayn at school. However, as the child of a mixed marriage he also found his early experiences of schooling to be challenging. 'I almost felt like I didn't fit in at my first two schools because I was the only mixed heritage kid in my class,' he wrote in the book *Dare to Dream: Life as One*

Direction. This made life uncomfortable and he eventually moved to a new school where he stood out less and settled in happily. It was here that he also began to note the charms of girls. The first time he kissed a girl, Zayn found that he had to improvise to make the smooch work. 'I was about eight, nine years old. [He has also speculated elsewhere he might have been ten when this happened.] I remember the girl being taller than me and we were outside somewhere so I had to stand on top of a brick to get level with her. That's a major thing I remember about my first kiss.' As he entered his teenage years, Zayn became more and more aware of the charms of the fairer sex, including famous females. 'My first celebrity crush was definitely Megan Fox,' he confessed. 'When I watched the *Transformers* movie she just looked ridiculously hot in that film.'

It is no coincidence that it was also about this time that Zayn began to take extra special care in his appearance. Having become fond of beautiful girls, he wanted to look his best. That said, his attention to detail exceeded that of most lads his age. 'Vain Zayn' would even happily sacrifice thirty minutes of sleep in the morning in order to have time to perfect his look and style his hair to his highly exacting standards. Perhaps living around so many females had influenced him to take such a keen interest in his appearance. It was actually his dad who cut Zayn's hair as a child and often it was he who helped Zayn get the look right in the morning. All of the attention that was being paid to Zayn's appearance paid off: he looked wonderful.

As he became more aware of girls, Zayn experimented with different looks to try and gain their attention and discover his own identity. At one stage he shaved his hair off and shaved lines into his eyebrows. As a fan of hip hop and R&B he was trying to look the part. His overall aim was to look 'cool' and 'hard'. With the benefit of hindsight he wonders if he ever managed either. He did attract the attention of girls and at the age of fifteen he got his first ever girlfriend. Prior to becoming famous he had only had three girlfriends. By then he had developed some basic tastes: chief among them is that he likes a girl with plenty of character and fun. To Zayn, those characteristics are more important than how a girl looks. Some details of his romantic life, though, will probably always remain secret. Asked when he lost his virginity, Zayn was teasingly evasive: 'a gentleman would never say'.

All the while, his love of singing and performing grew every year. He loved how it felt to perform: it made him come alive and placed him at the centre of everyone's attention. It also gave him an outlet for his huge level of energy. Indeed, Zayn was such an energetic child that Tricia had once taken him to the doctors to see if there was anything they could do to make him more serene.

At home, he performed mini gigs in front of his family, in which he sang songs by artists including Daniel Bedingfield. The youngster could not have known it at the time but one of Bedingfield's best-known fans is a certain Simon Cowell – the man who would eventually change Zayn's life.

As well as singing, Zayn found he had a flair for acting. At secondary school he got a part in a production of *Grease*. Due to his diminutive build, a new part had to be created for Zayn who was too small to play the lead, as Louis had done at his school. Zayn went on to take parts in other productions including the light-hearted gangster story *Bugsy Malone* – in which he landed the part of the lead – and the fantasy adventure *Arabian Nights*. He found playing the part of someone else, of effectively stepping into a new identity, to be both liberating and exhilarating. He got such a high from performing that sometimes it took him a while to 'come down' afterwards and relax enough to sleep. He was getting an early experience of something that hits lots of artists – the 'performance high'. At least he had new friends with whom to share the experience. He befriended several of his fellow performers and remains friends with many of them to this day. Despite his busy schedule, Zayn has done his best to stay grounded and he considers contact with his childhood friends to be a very easy and positive way of doing this.

Zayn does not conform to all the characteristics associated with 'middle born' children. For instance, many experts believe that such children will tend to excel more in non-academic ways, rather than at school. Zayn has excelled at both. At the age of eight he already had the reading age of an adult. He is also a keen artist – something he believes he inherited from his dad. Zayn has eleven GCSEs and even sat his English GCSE a year early, getting a grade A. He asked if he could re-sit it the following year, in the hope he could go one better and get an A* grade. He was not allowed to take the exam again, but having to settle for an A grade is not the worst situation to be in. He is definitely not just a pretty face.

As a Capricorn, Zayn is expected to be ambitious and humorous yet also shy and reserved. He has certainly shown signs of all these traits. Fans have marvelled at his ready wit in some situations, yet have noticed how he can be quieter at others. When he looks back over his childhood he remembers occasions where he wanted to be in the limelight and to have everyone's attention, yet he has also recalled times where he preferred to hide away alone in a quiet room. These contrasts make Zayn the intriguing, many dimensional person he is, and it is these complexities that help bring him that intangible but crucial quality for all those who wish to entertain: the x factor.

So, he was obviously a promising candidate for the ITV talent show of the same name. Having distinguished himself as a 'star' at Tong High, he put his sixth-form courses on temporary hold to audition for *The X Factor*. The assistant headteacher, Steve Gates, told local newspaper the *Telegraph and Argus* that Zayn was: 'A model student who excelled in all the performing arts subjects, one of the specialist subjects here at Tong'. He added: 'He was always a star performer in all the school productions.' It was a music teacher at Tong High who first suggested that Zayn enter the famous talent show. It took him some time to pluck up the courage to actually go through with the audition. At fifteen in 2008 – the same year that Liam Payne first auditioned, reaching the judges' houses phase – Zayn did obtain an application form but did not get as far as filling it in. The following year, he did the same. The desire to enter the show was strong, but it was surpassed by nerves. Did he really have what it took, he kept asking himself? He knew he looked great but wondered whether his voice would be strong enough and whether he had the nerve to see the contest through.

Finally, in 2010, he actually went for it. He filled in the form, sent it off and auditioned. Even then, though, he needed a final bit of encouragement. On the day of the audition he changed his mind again. Behind his doubt was a fear that he would be rejected. He wanted to stay in bed. Eventually it was his mum who ordered him to get up and go to the audition. 'I was really nervous but she told me just to get on with it and not miss my chance,' remembered Zayn.

Off he went. What happened next proved correct that well-worn maxim of family life: mother knows best.

4 NIALL HORAN

When One Direction stormed the charts in America, one of the first people to congratulate the boys on Twitter was the king of pop himself, Justin Bieber. After congratulating the whole band, the young Canadian heartthrob sent a follow-up Tweet to Niall Horan's account, which read: 'Good guys always win, bro.' This was a particularly apt message, for not only is Niall a long-term admirer of Bieber, the young Irishman is also one of life's good guys. Loyal, friendly and ever so witty, Niall has always been a bundle of joy to those who have encountered him. Bieber is far from alone in his appreciation, for Niall does not lack for champions to delight in his ongoing victories.

So, what was this Irish lad's childhood like? When asked to describe the Horan family,

Niall's father probably put it best: 'We were just ordinary people'. Niall Timothy Horan was born on 13 September 1993. He grew up in the town of Mullingar, in Westmeath, Ireland. The town he was raised in is small and quiet: as Niall himself puts it, there's not much for young people to do there. After all, its main tourist attractions are its lakes, and lakes – even stunningly beautiful ones – are only of limited interest to most teenagers. That said, Niall has remained staunchly loyal to the neighbourhood since he became inter-nationally famous. He still believes that the best way to spend an evening is to go out in Mullingar with his best friends. There might not be that much to do, but there is no place like home and no friends like the ones you made as a kid.

The town is rather proud of Niall in return – there have even been calls for a statue of him to be erected there. On a wider level, he is proud to be an Irishman and to fly the flag for Ireland on the world stage. The only part of that experience that disquiets him is when people make ignorant remarks about Ireland and the Irish. For instance, he has complained that people constantly ask him if he likes potatoes – in reference to the Irish potato famine. Although Niall now travels the world through his work, leading an enviable life, he still feels there is no place like his home nation. As his childhood friend Sean Cullen observed, even in the midst of so much fame, success and attention, if there is one thing Niall enjoys is a chance to touch base with his buddies back where he grew up. 'He loves coming home,' said Cullen of his friend.

For the first four years of his life Niall's family lived in the centre of the town. Then they moved to an estate further out of town but soon after the move Niall's parents split up. It was a very upsetting time for him and all of the Horan family. However, Niall was young when this happened, so his understanding of the emotional and practical complexities of it would have been looser. At first he stayed with his mother but then moved in with his dad, whose home was located more conveniently for Niall's school. His early memories include playing on the street with his older brother and other kids. These were not always harmonious times for the siblings, as Niall was always the quintessential younger brother. He was not only younger in years, he was always short for his age, which only added to his vulnerable air.

Not that this stopped the plucky Niall from once striking his brother Greg with a table tennis bat, drawing blood in the process. Some of the toys that Niall enjoyed playing with as a child included a toy tractor, which he drove up and down the street, and an army outfit with a helmet and a huge toy gun. Then, one Christmas, he got a Scalextric track. 'I must have been about four or five years old and I got a Scalextric thing and that was probably one of the best presents I ever got,' he told Capital Radio. They had pet goldfish that they named after the cartoon characters Tom and Jerry. Unfortunately Greg overfed them and they died – an upsetting experience for all concerned. There was often tension between the two brothers as they grew up. Niall has said that for many years they 'hated each other' but they are now fond and loving siblings.

Further early memories Niall has of life include playing in his toy tractor, travelling to New York for a family holiday and crying on the first day of school. He quickly found his confidence at school and became a very cheeky schoolboy. Full of fun and chatter, he says he 'talked a lot during lessons' but never so much that he got into any serious trouble, apart from on one occasion when he bunked a day off – and landed himself in a great deal of trouble.

His favourite subjects were Geography and French; he was less keen on English and Maths. Homework was a part of school life that he never quite learned to enjoy. One of his closest school friends was a lad called Nicky – they first befriended each other when Nicky broke wind during a boring geography class. The parp really broke the monotony of the lesson. Nicky could not have known at the time of the significance of his untimely fart, which led to a lasting friendship with a future internationally famous pop star. It was an eruption with considerable consequence.

All the while, Niall's love of music, the tool that would take him to such renown, was growing. He learned to play the recorder soon after he started school and his musical ways continued to develop from there. The first person to note that he had a good singing voice was his singing teacher at primary school, Mrs Caulfield. Having heard Niall's beautiful voice during Christmas carol services, she put him forward for the local town's choir. He was eight years of age. His love of – and talent for – singing was also being noticed by his family. Once, during a road trip with his auntie in Galway, he was sitting in the back of the car singing a song by the crooner Garth Brooks. So good was his singing that his auntie told him she had thought the radio was on. From that moment, she believed that her nephew was going to become a pop star.

As Niall has reflected, a similar car-based experience befell the world-famous singer Michael Bublé when he was a child. A keen student of other artists' careers, Niall was thrilled by the coincidence. Little could he have known that he would one day meet his hero. As well as being inspired by Bublé's career, Niall has also studied the music and life of Frank Sinatra. Without Sinatra's example, he has said, he would not have become a singer himself. It is touching to remember that Niall, a young man who is now inspiring so many people, was in turn himself inspired in the past. He has long dreamed of a duet with his hero Justin Bieber – and that prospect doesn't seem so unlikely, given where Niall is now.

Two years after he joined the town choir, Niall took his love of singing and performing to a new level. 'I've always sung and when I was about ten, I played Oliver in the school play and I just always remember being really happy on stage,' he said. As well as singing and acting he was also learning to play the guitar. Niall's strumming has become a key part of his place within One Direction. He was twelve when he began to learn to play the instrument. 'He learned how to play from the internet,' remembered his father, Robert. With his voice and guitar technique improving, he then entered some talent shows. Among the songs he sang were 'I'm Yours' by Jason Mraz, 'Last Request' by Paolo Nutini and 'The Man Who Can't Be Moved' by The Script. Sometimes he entered the contests alongside his friend Kieron, who would accompany Niall's singing with some neat guitar playing.

They made for an impressive duo. The first

talent show they took part in was a local affair. Niall, then thirteen, was noticed by the local media at the event and he got his first taste of publicity when they ran articles and photographs featuring him. It felt strange, but exciting, to see his name and face in print. He felt real pride when he saw the reaction to this from his family and friends. The next show he entered he won. He had sung Chris Brown's song 'With You'. His victory gave him sufficient confidence to believe that he could have a future as a professional singer. Further local media coverage followed his participation in a regional *Stars In Their Eyes*-style show at the Mullingar Arts Centre. He had really enjoyed the experience and his confidence was growing. Could, he wondered, his auntie be right? Was he destined to become a pop idol like his heroes?

Soon, he got to perform actual live slots as a support act. One of these was when he opened for 2009 *X Factor* finalist Lloyd Daniels. Niall had been impressed by heartthrob Daniels' experience on the show and told the young Welshman that he was planning to enter himself. Daniels would later claim that he had encouraged Niall to do so, but Niall remembered the exchange differently.

As he remembered it, the baby-faced Daniels actually seemed less than impressed when he stated his plan.

As well as performing, Niall loved listening to music: one of his favourite bands was Westlife. He also became a fan of Justin Bieber and really loves the Jonas Brothers – 'they are legends', he says. Little could he know as he enjoyed their music that he would one day meet both of them and then go on to begin to emulate their enormous success.

Niall has had a less eventful love life than some other members of One Direction, but he has still had his encounters with the fairer sex. He had his first kiss when he was eleven. It was with a foreign exchange student who was visiting from France. She was boarding with the family of one of Niall's friends. He developed a crush on several female celebrities including Jennifer Lopez. 'Who can resist that bum?' he has wondered aloud. He also had a girlfriend around the age of thirteen, but says it was not a long-term or serious deal. 'I've not actually been on too many dates,' he has told *OK!* magazine. 'I just like sitting at home, chilling and watching a movie,' he added.

Other memorable moments from Niall's childhood included football matches on the school fields and a host of memorable hairstyles that he now cringes at. Well, neither of those pastimes ever did David Beckham any harm. As for Niall, his parents have both summed him up succinctly. 'He's a lighthearted lad. One thing I do know is that he is completely committed and focused on his singing,' said his mother Maura. 'He'd sing for his breakfast, dinner and tea.' Lighthearted is exactly what Niall usually is. Indeed, there are very few things that can ruffle his easy-going nature. One thing that can, though, is pigeons, which he took against after a hair-raising experience while he was answering the call of nature. 'I can't stand them after one once flew in through my bathroom window and went for me while I was having a wee. That was enough. I think pigeons target me' he told the *Sun*. Well, why should they be any different to One Direction's millions of fans?

As for his father, Robert, he says that Niall had shown glimpses of other entertainment skills early in life. 'Niall was always interested in showbiz,' he told the *Irish Independent*. 'Apart from singing, he always spent his childhood mimicking others. He's brilliant, he'd have been a stand-up comedian if he hadn't gone down this route. He can pick up any dialect.' Niall is frequently the most humorous and entertaining member of One Direction. His funny ways are a longstanding character trait of the cheeky lad. When the band is working hard on the road, it is often Niall's wit that keeps them going.

When he needs to be, however, Niall can be very serious. Don't let the cheeky face fool you: he has steely ambition in his soul. Even as he applied to audition for *The X Factor*, Niall, having been inspired by the success of teenage winner Joe McElderry, seemed to have a sense that he was going to go places. So much so even though he was dating a girl who he found 'amazing', he decided to break up with her shortly before he auditioned for *The X Factor*, believing that his life was about to change dramatically. 'I needed to concentrate on my career,' he said.

His mum, Maura, has spoken more about this girl and her relationship with Niall. 'He had a girlfriend at home, from his school days, before he auditioned for *The X Factor*,' she told the *Herald*. 'But then he was doing that and she was doing exams, so life is very different for him now. I don't know if he sees much of her when he's home, she was lovely, but they were only sixteen at the time – there's never anything too steady about a relationship at that age.' The fact he ended the relationship shows that Niall clearly was not just auditioning for the hell of it – he meant business. That said, he still had the nous to develop some other plans to fall back on in case he did not succeed in the talent show. Having recently finished his GCSE exams at Colaiste Mhuire, he had plans to go to university to study Civil Engineering. However, he is unlikely to follow up on that plan anytime soon. The nice guy of pop has bigger fish to fry nowadays.

5 LIAM PAYNE

If there is a single quality that has shaped
the course of Liam Payne's life to date it is
determination. Not just any sort of determination
– but gritty, steely resolve. Liam can have fun
and melt hearts when the time is right, but he
will not let anything get in his way as he seeks
to fulfil his goals. Which is just as well because,
like many stars, he has had to overcome several
setbacks in his journey to the top. The most
significant and challenging of them all is that
he was, as he has himself put it, born 'effectively
dead'. Doctors had to work fast to bring him
round – a far from ideal start. He arrived into
the world on 29 August 1993, a full three weeks
prematurely, and then suffered from a series of
health issues during the first four years of his
life. The fundamental problem he faced was that

he was born with just one functioning kidney. This occurs in about one out of 750 people and creates a number of complications for the sufferer.

When he was born the doctors could get no reaction from him and feared he had been stillborn. Luckily, he survived this dramatic entrance to the world but he was still destined for several years of regular hospital visits. At first the doctors did not know why he kept falling sick. He went in and out of hospital for tests and examinations as doctors tried to get to the bottom of the problem. Finally, after several years of regular examinations, the doctors discovered Liam's kidney issue. Although, like most people, Liam has two kidneys, only one of them worked properly, and in the years in which his misfunctioning kidney had been undetected it had become so scarred that there was no hope of saving it and turning it into a healthy, working organ.

Instead, Liam was sentenced to a course of treatment that would be enough to take any lad to the brink of despair. At one stage he had to have no less than thirty-two injections into his arm each morning and evening. He must have felt like a pincushion as he underwent this painful and time-consuming treatment. As anyone who has undergone complicated medical treatment as a child remembers, the desire for the treatment to be finished and consigned to the past is strong. More than anything, the child just wants to be normal like other children. But despite this, he managed to stay cheery most of the time, and his mum remembers him dancing round the sitting room to the theme tune from the children's television series *Noddy*.

Eventually, the treatment was scaled back and Liam's life became more normal. He was told that due to his kidney problem it was more important than ever that he keep himself as healthy as possible. For instance, he had to take care not to drink too much liquid; even water had to be carefully rationed. He took all the advice the doctors gave him very seriously, and the legacy of that advice has been a considerable factor in everything that has happened in his life ever since. It has kept Liam more focused than most on leading a healthy, successful and long life.

His first school was Collingwood Infants School, on Collingwood Road in Bushbury, Wolverhampton. Few who were there at the same time will forget Liam in a hurry as, within days of arriving, he got himself into plenty of mischief. He was in and out of the headmistress's office after a number of capers, including water fights. He also climbed onto the roof to retrieve footballs that had been accidentally kicked up there by over-zealous strikers. Although he could be playful and impish, Liam did concentrate in class. One of his favourite subjects was science.

While he was at primary school he also began to develop a love of music and singing – a love that would eventually change his life forever. When he was just five years of age, Liam gave his first public performance. 'I've always loved singing, it's something I've always done, ever since I first got up on karaoke when I was at holiday camp and mumbled the words to Robbie Williams' "Let Me Entertain You"', he explained later. Although his Robbie rendition had not been a pitch-perfect affair, Liam definitely enjoyed it – and the reaction he got – and it made him want to continue developing his voice. His mother was not bothered by the imperfections: she was so proud that she filmed the performance. He has also spoken of another early karaoke performance, in which he sang R Kelly's 'I Believe I Can Fly'.

Back in the family home, he had plenty of love. His father, Geoff, and mother, Karen, had also produced two daughters, Nicola and Ruth, both of whom are older than Liam. They, too, enjoy singing. Nicola is the eldest of the siblings. To Liam she was an authority figure with an almost parental air. As the youngest sibling, Liam is a 'last born' child. Experts who have studied the effect that a child's birth order in a family has on them have identified a number of characteristics that are common in last borns, among which are extra reserves of charm and a strong desire to be centre of attention. Such children are also often strongly creative, but less ambitious and organized than others. They are said to be rebellious and willing to take risks.

How much of this can we see in Liam? Clearly, his charm is undeniable. He supplements his physical good looks with an allure and charisma that comes from deeper in his soul. As for a desire to be centre of attention, he has this only partially. Clearly, he is comfortable under the spotlight of the stage and television cameras. However, in more everyday social situations he can be relatively shy and introverted. Now, many have identified him as 'the quiet one' of the band. Is he rebellious, creative and risk-taking? As we shall see, yes, he is. However, one last-born characteristic that could not apply less to Liam is a lack of ambition. More than any member of One Direction, Liam has a clearly set objective that he has been focused on for several years.

Indeed, so ambitious is he that he has had more than one goal in his life and had considered a number of different career paths before he turned to music, more than one of which was of a sporting bent. He tried – and failed – to get into the school football teams so, instead, decided to try out running. His first attempt was a cross-country run and to his delight Liam both enjoyed the feeling of running and also came first in the race.

This sweet feeling was temporarily soured when Liam was accused, quite unfairly, of cheating. He had been up against one of the region's finest athletes, someone who onlookers were amazed that Liam, a mere newcomer, had managed to beat. The following week, Liam challenged the same runner to a repeat contest. Again, Liam beat him. Now there could be no doubt about his ability. He quickly became a fanatical runner. He loved it all: the feeling of freedom in the open air, the fact it kept him fit, the sense of achievement and the natural high he felt at the end of a race. He joined the Wolverhampton and Bilston Athletics Club. He was truly committed to running and would frequently rise as early as six a.m. to run up to six miles before school, as well as another couple of miles in the early evening.

All the training paid off. By the time he was twelve, Liam had become such an accomplished and successful runner that he was put in his school's under-eighteen team. Here he was, not yet a teenager, competing successfully with men of eighteen years of age. At his club, Liam continued to compete too, and for three years he finished in the top three for his age group in 1,500-metre runs. As Liam himself said, these achievements are 'amazing'. He came agonizingly close to a place in the England running team. It is quite possible that, had he got that place, we would know him not as a member of One Direction, but as a member of Team GB at the London 2012 Olympics.

Running was just one sporting pastime that Liam was taking part in. Thanks to regular family holidays in America he had become a basketball fan. He joined a local team but soon found himself targeted by some older boys who were jealous of Liam's snazzy American kit. However, the bullying went beyond just nasty words: Liam became so scared and upset that he shared his concerns with his family. One of his sisters was dating a former boxer at the time, and Liam's parents suggested that he also learn to box, so the bullies would think twice about picking on him in the future.

Often, people who have kidney problems are advised to avoid contact sports but Liam was cleared to try out boxing. Once he got to the boxing club he was thrown in at the deep end: one of his first fights, at the age of twelve, was against a thirty-eight-year-old boxing trainer.

No wonder his early visits to the boxing club were such scary experiences for Liam. He would often arrive home shaken-up and bruised – he even suffered a broken nose and a perforated eardrum. But he still kept going: most weeks he was there three times.

However, fighting skills aside, he was also gaining the very thing he had gone there for: confidence. The bullies continued to be nasty to him for a while, including chasing him down the street one day. These were cowards in every sense: they were older than Liam and acted in a pack. When Liam's patience snapped he had a fight with one of them and, thanks to his boxing training, he emerged the winner. He got in lots of trouble, at school in the aftermath, with expulsion being one of the options he was threatened with. He had shown the world that he was not to be easily pushed around, though.

Other sports that Liam enjoyed included football, as both a player and a fan – despite his disappointment at not making it into the school team. From taking part in lunch-hour 'kickabouts' to watching West Bromwich Albion at The Hawthorns, he has always been a true, passionate devotee of the beautiful game. When his favourite team was promoted, he joined his fellow supporters to run onto the pitch in celebration – 'a great moment' as he recalled. He also appreciated PE lessons. In fact, he so enjoyed them that it was suggested to Liam that he could consider becoming a PE teacher. It was an option that was of some interest to him.

Liam always seemed to be looking to his future. While he cherished the experience of being a kid he also had an eye on what was to come. Other career paths he considered included an apprenticeship at the aircraft factory where his father worked. Liam imagined it would be a bit like playing giant Lego games all day, though his Dad was quick to tell him that in fact it was very tough work. Perhaps I could be a fireman, thought Liam, his imagination racing as ever. He might even have fancied his chances of becoming a businessman. Having watched the BBC business series *Dragon's Den*, Liam became so inspired by its entrepreneurs that he started a small venture of his own. He would buy large packets of sweets and then sell them at school for a profit. The dragons of the den would surely have been impressed: young Liam frequently made a profit of around £50 a week.

In fact, his childhood business experiences have given Liam a fixed view on how young people should conduct their lives. They have formed some political opinions in his mind. 'Young people should stay in school and get qualifications,' he told *The Sunday Times*. 'You can't just sit around doing nothing. They should get out there and make things happen,' says Liam. 'Flog stuff on eBay.' He is not the only One Direction member to admire and favour young enterprise. Harry, too, has spoken out in similar terms. He said of young people: 'They should become entrepreneurs, make a job for themselves, start a company.'

Liam went through several hairstyles as a kid. These included a number three crop, a tramlines style and what he called 'a big mushroom'. Eventually he settled on the popular fringe. He began to notice the charms of girls as he grew up, and had his first kiss at the age of eleven. 'It was with a girl called Vicky – she was a lovely little girl,' he recalled. 'Good stuff – early starter', he added. He also recalled a girl called Charnelle who used to send him love letters. She was two years older than him and Liam thought himself quite the grown-up, dating an older girl. None of these girls knew they were encountering a future star who would soon become a heartthrob to girls across the planet.

He developed a huge crush on a girl called Emily and asked her out over twenty times before she said yes. He only secured the positive response after singing to her. The song he chose was Mario's 'Let Me Love You'. 'She dumped me the next day because I had pressured her into it by singing to her.' It may surprise some of his fans to learn that before he was famous, Liam, now adored by millions of girls worldwide, was actually quite often unlucky in love. Sometimes he was told by friends that a particular girl was keen on him. It was after he confidently asked the girl out only to be turned down that he would discover his friends had just been pranking him. 'Mortifying', was how he put it. Asked by *The Sunday Times* when he lost his virginity, 'I can't remember', was his playfully discreet reply.

Meanwhile, music was still a big part of Liam's life. That primary school performance of 'Let Me

Entertain You' had proved to be just the start of his love affair with music. He certainly enjoyed listening to it – his favourite acts included Robbie Williams and Oasis, the lyrics of the latter act chiming with Liam's outlook on life. 'You've gotta make it happen,' sing Oasis on one of their tracks. Liam agreed. As well as listening to music, he also enjoyed singing, having joined the school choir when he was in Year Nine. With the choir Liam got plenty of experience of singing in front of an audience. They even set a world record when they and several other schools joined together to sing the same song – 'Lean On Me' by Bill Withers – in unison.

Actually, he could not stop singing. During family outings he would sing in the car and then at home he would don a pair of sunglasses and croon along to his dad's Oasis CDs. Showing his natural sense of performance, Liam would copy the posture of the band's lead singer Liam Gallagher: hands tucked behind the back, neck tipped so the face pointed upwards. In those moments he did his best to imagine what it would be like to actually perform a concert in front of thousands of fanatical fans. Liam's other big inspiration is American singer Usher, the man who helped launch the career of Justin Bieber, to whom Liam would be compared when his own career began.

Always the sort of lad to take his interests to the next level, when he was twelve, Liam joined a local performing arts group called Pink Productions. His teacher there, Jodie Richards, remembered her encounters with the future heartthrob. 'Liam joined us as a timid boy who wanted to sing after watching his sisters perform with us,' she told the *Express & Star* newspaper. She never doubted his talent but found that he needed an injection of confidence to match it. 'Who'd have thought the Liam we see today would have nearly had to be forced onto the stage? It was clear very early that Liam was a natural talent.' She added that he gained more and more confidence with each show and tackled some 'big singing numbers'. Assessing him as an overall character she described him as 'such a lovely lad' and explained how 'very proud' she is to be able to say she knows him.

He continued to take any chance he could to do more karaoke slots. Indeed, having sung karaoke in America, England, Spain and Portugal, Liam had almost performed a world tour of sorts long before One Direction had been formed. Through these performances and others Liam became gradually more accomplished. His voice improved and so did his overall stage presence. (Of all the future members of One Direction, Liam would make best use of the stage at his first 2010 *X Factor* audition.) That confidence onstage was honed during these regular performances in the years leading up to it.

Liam listened to the feedback he was given and perfected his persona. When he first entered the show in 2008 his friends teased him but it was only ever banter. At heart, they wish him the best. He got more and more excited as the big date grew closer. He so wanted to do well. 'People had told me that I was a good singer so I thought I would give it a go and audition for *X Factor*,' he said.

That said, for a boy who would go on to become an international heartthrob, Liam certainly chose an 'interesting' outfit for his first television appearance. He wore a shirt that was too big for him, making the collar appear almost comically oversized, underneath a waistcoat. His jeans were also too big for him so he had to tie his belt really tight just to hold them up. Although viewers were unaware that one of the shoes he was wearing had a hole in it, that fact only added to Liam's discomfort as he queued for many hours to get his chance to sing in front of Simon Cowell, Cheryl Cole and Louis Walsh.

He did not let his peculiar clothing combination dent his confidence and arrived in the audition room looking very composed and self-confident. 'I'm here to win,' he told the judges, throwing down the gauntlet from the off. 'A lot of people have told me I'm a good singer and that I've got the X Factor – but I don't really know what the X Factor is and I believe you guys do.' It was a measured and shrewd opening line. Simon Cowell, in particular, admires those whose ambitions are high, but equally dislikes any sense of delusion or desperation. Liam had pitched himself well. Afterwards, Liam said he felt 'a bit nervous' before he started singing, but then the nerves disappeared. He sang the song

'Fly Me to the Moon', clicking the beat with his fingers and even at one point winking cheekily at Cheryl Cole. She appreciated the moment and beamed back in approval.

All in all, it had been a more than adequate performance. When it was time for the judges' verdicts, it was Cowell's opinion that Liam was most interested in. He was more than a little in awe of the head judge and was dying to receive his widely coveted nod of approval – and he knew that Cowell did not offer praise lightly. It was Cowell who spoke first, saying he saw 'potential' in Liam but simultaneously felt he lacked 'a bit of grit, a bit of emotion'. Cole said she liked Liam and, in contrast to Cowell, was impressed by the 'charisma' he showed. Louis Walsh, too, was charmed by the youngster. 'I think he could do really well,' said the Irishman.

Cowell then spoke again. He told Liam he is 'a young guy, good looking – people will like you', but added that there was 'twenty per cent missing for me at the moment'. Here, Liam's self-assurance came to the fore. Rather than buckling under Cowell's observation, he rose to the occasion. 'Well, give me another audition and I'll show you I've got that twenty per cent,' he said. Cole was visibly impressed by this plucky answer, which Liam had delivered with just the right balance of confidence and politeness. When it came to the vote, all three judges said 'yes' – Liam had done it! He left the room and was mobbed by his family.

Moving forward, Liam showed his maturity when he continued to take Cowell's criticism in the constructive spirit in which it had been offered. '[Cowell's feedback] gave me something to work on, which is good,' he said. Given that some contestants much older than Liam threw huffs and tantrums when they were criticized by the panel, Liam's mature reaction to it becomes all the more admirable.

The next stage in his journey was the boot camp phase of the show. Here, Liam got the chance to mingle with more fellow hopefuls. His ambitious instinct told him that it was worth chatting to as many people as possible. He turned out to be quite the networker. 'People think it's just a singing competition but it's so much more than that,' he said, explaining how much he had enjoyed the overall experience, particularly the chance to make so many new friends.

Then he sang onstage in front of the judges, and gave it his all. The judges were impressed. 'Very convincing, very professional and you're only fourteen,' Walsh told him. 'Liam, you're a little dark horse,' added Cowell, prompting a proud yet bashful smile from Liam. Later, the contestants were gathered as the first dreaded chop of boot camp was delivered. Although many of the contestants were extremely anxious as they waited to find out if they had survived the chop, Liam said he felt 'confident'.

Once again, his instinct was spot on – he was through to the next stage of boot-camp. He was, he recalled, 'slightly more nervous' on this day. He sang Elton John's 'Your Song'. Putting emotion and drama into the performance, he delivered the song with moments of light theatre, wanting the judges to see the full range of his abilities and to show Cowell that the 'missing twenty per cent' had been found. After finishing his song, Liam had to leave the stage and let the judges decide their verdict. When he had gone, Cowell told his fellow judges, 'I like him'.

With Cowell's verdict always so weighty, it seemed to viewers who watched this episode that Liam would be safely through to the next, all-important, judges' houses phase. However, it was not to be that simple. Instead, the first major twist of the series was to engulf Liam. First, the contestants were called to the stage in groups, where they lined up and listened as the judges told them whether they had made it through to the next stage, or whether they would be going home. As is customary, the judges injected as much drama as possible into these moments. One favourite trick is to tell the contestants 'It's bad news' only to add, following an agonizing pause, a follow-up statement such as, 'You'll have to put up with us a bit longer, as you're through!'

When Liam stood alongside his fellow contestants, he listened intently to Cowell's words. 'Whatever happens, you can leave with your heads held high,' the head judge told them, but added: 'It's bad news'. Even as they left the stage, Liam momentarily turned back to the judges. Perhaps he was hoping for a last-moment twist. Backstage, he was distraught. He said he thought he had done enough to progress, and said: 'I feel like something's been taken away from me.' The judges were then shown changing their minds about Liam. 'I'm telling you, I think this kid's got a shot,' said Cowell. He then ruled that they would put Liam through after all. 'I promise you, this is the right decision,' he said. The others were happy to go along with it.

A producer approached Liam and told him the judges wanted him to return to the stage. Naturally, he looked shocked. He had watched past series of the show and knew that there were always a few 'shock twists' to ramp up the drama. While he hoped he was returning to the stage to be told he was back in the competition, he knew he could not afford to count on anything. Cowell broke the silence when Liam appeared on the stage, looking a little sheepish. 'I don't often do this, but it was such a close call,' Cowell began. Liam then interrupted to make a final plea for himself: 'I want to take it all the way, Simon'.

'I know you do,' Cowell replied. 'And the other thing I want to say to you is: we've changed our minds.' Liam was so shocked and overjoyed he sank straight to his knees. 'I'd have really really been mad if I had gone home and not done this,' said Cowell. Amazing stuff: Liam was the 'comeback kid'! He had already phoned home to tell them he was out, so when he made a second call to tell his family that he was, in fact, through to judges' houses, they took some convincing. 'No, I'm being serious – I got through! I'm being super serious,' he said. What a rollercoaster day it had been. A touching moment came when Liam's fellow contestants were seen cheering him on. He had won over more than the judges at boot camp.

From believing his *X Factor* journey was over, Liam was now being told of the arrangements for his trip to Barbados to sing in front of Simon Cowell in the judges' houses stage. He knew there was hard work to come, but he also knew that if he got through this stage he would be through to the live shows. The fact that his category was being mentored by his favourite judge only added to Liam's excitement. His category was very strong, including a cheeky-faced Irish boy called Eoghan Quigg and other major contenders including Austin Drage and Scott Bruton.

Alongside Cowell in Barbados was his long-term sidekick Sinitta. She appeared before Liam and the other boys wearing a golden swimsuit that left little to the imagination. 'What are you *wearing*?' asked Cowell. Everyone had a good chuckle and then it was time to be serious. Liam was asked how nervous he felt and he insisted he felt fine. He was again proving remarkably mature for a boy his age. He played around with a basketball during some spare time in Barbados. He reflected that he had something in common with Troy, the character that Zac Efron plays in *High School Musical*. Like Troy, Liam was attempting to balance a love of basketball with a love of singing. 'The story of *High School Musical* is basically my story,' he said. He sang the Take That ballad 'A Million Love Songs' and, as his second song, 'Hero' by Enrique Iglesias. Dressed all in white, he looked every inch the part of an angelic pop star. After he finished, Sinitta seemed smitten. 'Love him,' she said. 'He has such a cute face – nice little voice as well.'

After the performance Liam said he was sure he had done all he could. 'I'm happy with that – I'll settle for that,' he said. There was then a long night ahead for Liam and the other contestants. They had to sit and wait while, safely out of their earshot, Cowell and Sinitta narrowed down the six remaining contestants to the three who would go through to the live shows. Liam described the feeling as he waited as one of numbness. Reflecting on what he had been through, he said that as he had passed each stage his desire was only strengthened. 'I kept thinking: I want this more, I want this more,' he said.

However, then came the decision, and Cowell told Liam: 'You look almost like the perfect pop star. I've made a decision – it's bad news.' Again, Liam tried to argue his case. This time, though, there would be no respite – he was out. Cowell admitted to *Xtra Factor* presenter Holly Willoughby afterwards that he had 'teetered on the edge' of putting Liam through. When Liam watched the show later he drew significant comfort from learning how close he had come, but he still found the rejection very difficult to take. He went home and started to pick-up the pieces. Cowell had advised him to go and take his GCSEs, continue to work on his singing, and then return in two years. Liam set about preparing to do just that. He launched a website to promote himself and put himself about for any live singing slots he could get.

He had certainly captured the public imagination. Schoolgirls had swooned over his good looks, while both his voice and determination had impressed lots of viewers. The day after the judges' houses phase was broadcast he was invited onto Lorraine Kelly's morning ITV show to discuss his experiences on *The X Factor*. Reflecting on his experience of visiting Barbados overall, Liam quipped: 'Well, it was all right until I sunburnt me feet,' adding that he had tried to be careful with the sun cream but that it had 'never occurred' to him that his feet could burn.

Kelly asked him who he thought might go on to win the series. In his answer, he showed breath-taking understanding of the pop market. Singling out boy band JLS as strong candidates for victory, he said: 'There's no black group currently – there's a gap in the market for one. They're a bit like Boyz II Men so they've got the international edge.' JLS emerged runners-up at the end of the series, but the scale of their success made them considered the *de facto* winners. It was amazing that Liam, then fifteen, had so accurately and wisely assessed their appeal and prospects.

Liam's disappointment at being sent home was still palpable and could not be avoided or ignored. 'It was so close – it was hard to take,' he told Lorraine Kelly. She commented on his overall confidence during his time in the competition and he said he put it down to the fact that he enjoyed singing – so why be nervous about something he enjoyed? As is often the case with his pronouncements, this was straightforward common sense. He said he would 'love to' reapply for the 2009 series. (As it turned out, this would not be possible, as the lower age limit would be raised back to sixteen for 2009 and he would still be fifteen at the crucial cut-off point.)

Still, he certainly planned to return before long and was hopeful that he could go further next time. He pointed out that the 2008 *Britain's Got Talent* teenage winner, George Sampson, had to go through two series of the show before he emerged as the winner. For Liam, this was a huge encouragement. 'If it takes me two goes, it take me two goes,' he said. Comparing his first *X Factor* experience to 'the coursework' he predicted that his second go would be like an exam. 'All I've got to do now,' he said, looking forward already to his second stab at *The X Factor*, 'is pass the exam'.

He would do so – with flying colours.

6 IT'S TIME TO FACE THE MUSIC!

The X Factor has faced many controversies and criticisms since its first episode on 4 September 2004. Most recently it has faced rival shows that have attempted to knock it off its lofty perch. However, at the time of writing at least, it remains Britain's leading talent show and one that makes an almost grotesque amount of revenue for all parties concerned. True to the drama that its boss Cowell likes to engender in the programme itself, as a franchise it has had its ups and downs. It has as many elephants in its graveyard as it does successful graduates. Nowadays, one of its proudest boasts is that it launched the career of One Direction.

Before all of which, the show was conceived, created and launched by Simon Cowell. He had first come to fame – and infamy – on the reality show *Pop Idol*, which was launched in 2001. Previously unknown outside of the inner circles of the British record industry, Cowell quickly distinguished himself as the show's 'Mr Nasty', speaking with such fearsome honesty and wit that he quickly became the star of the show. Some hated him for his frankness, others loved him for it – but nobody was ignoring him. Over two series of *Pop Idol* he became a national celebrity. His fame was then extended to the United States where his withering put-downs on *American Idol* shocked and delighted viewers more accustomed to relentless positivity and political correctness.

Meanwhile, back in Britain, Cowell was enjoying his fame but was also plotting how to take things one step further. As a judge on *Pop Idol* he had become famous but his financial ambitions know no bounds and he devised *The X Factor* – a series on which he would not only judge, but also own and run the show. It has launched the careers of artists as successful as Leona Lewis, Alexandra Burke, G4, Olly Murs and JLS. True, there have also been some flops, including Steve Brookstein and Leon Jackson. Other finalists, such as Joe McElderry, have stuttered before finding a degree of fame, their success coming as much in spite of, as because of, their association with the show.

Of the several significant differences between *Pop Idol* and *The X Factor*, the most pertinent to One Direction is the fact that in the latter show bands are allowed to audition. This gives *The X Factor* a new dimension. That said, bands have not always found the experience to be plain sailing. With reality television contests so focused on the often dramatic background stories of their competitors, bands have found it difficult to create suitable intensity around themselves. While some bands made a success of the show – most notably the aforementioned G4 and JLS who both finished runners-up in their respective series – many found that they were voted out very quickly once the live shows began. It was only in the 2011 series that a band actually won the show, in the form of the girl band Little Mix. This was a band that had been assembled during the series, in front of the viewers' eyes. The judges and producers had judged that several girls who had auditioned separately as solo singers would be best if they formed into a band. It was this very tactic that had brought together One Direction.

Each member of the band auditioned as a separate act in 2010. As we have seen, for some of them this was not their first brush with the series. The band member with the most significant history with the show was, of course, Liam Payne. We left him in the previous chapter recovering from the knockback he received in the 2008 series. He was channelling that disappointment into something positive: a renewed bid to make it as a solo pop star. He still wanted to be the next Robbie Williams. Thanks to the momentary low-level fame his 2008 *X Factor* experience had offered him, he had something to build on. But he was not done with *The X Factor* yet: in fact, he was determined to give the talent show another crack. Even the concerns of some friends and family members – who feared Liam would be devastated if he was rejected again – was not enough to stop him.

A journalist on a local paper, who met with Liam in the run-up to his 2010 audition, described the way he had successfully updated his image. The journalist recalls him 'looking more like a star, rocking trendy tops, skinny jeans and a super-styled hairdo'. He had worked hard between the two auditions, both academically and musically. He sat eleven GCSEs at St Peter's Collegiate School and then moved on to study music technology at Wolverhampton College's Paget Road campus. He had made quite a few public performances off the back of his participation in the 2008 *X Factor* series, including one in front of 29,000 fans at Molineux Stadium, the home of Wolverhampton Wanderers Football Club. That performance came on the occasion of the team's home match against Manchester United. Surprisingly, he had even, with more than a little audacity, appointed men he described as 'managers' to guide his fledgling career.

After queuing up to re-audition in 2010, Liam was a natural choice to be interviewed and featured on-screen. Many viewers remembered him from last time round and, in any case, *The X Factor* has always enjoyed a returning contestant, they add to the 'soap opera' feel Simon Cowell likes to engender on the show.

Liam was asked about his rejection in Barbados. 'I think Simon made the right decision, it has given me the time to work on what I do,' he said. 'Doing the live shows when I was fifteen, I think I would have struggled to cope. I had never been on a big stage but now I have much more experience and I am really thankful to Simon for allowing me that. Everything happens for a reason. I'm now a lot more grown up and have performed in front of big audiences.'

That said, he was not denying that the rejection had hit hard. 'It was gutting,' he explained, 'I know what it's like to be thrown out.' Openly stating his priority for this audition, he admitted there was one man he wanted to impress most. He said it would 'mean the world' to be given a yes vote by Cowell. And it was Cowell whom Liam first addressed on taking the stage. 'How you doing, Simon, you all right?' he asked casually. 'Haven't seen you in a long time!' He then confirmed it had been two years since he last auditioned, at which point he 'made it through to Simon's house in Barbados'. He was coming across as very relaxed and confident. Inside, though, he was not quite so placid. In fact, he wrote later, he actually found being up on the stage in front of the judges a bit 'bizarre' and 'surreal'. He told the panel that he was going to sing 'Cry Me a River'. Cole assumed he meant the Justin Timberlake song, but within seconds the opening chords of the Michael Bublé track rang out.

At the end of the song he got a standing ovation from both the audience and the judging panel – even, he was particularly delighted to note, Simon Cowell had got to his feet, a rare and significant occurrence. Liam was stunned – he almost burst into tears there and then, as his emotions bubbled over. He composed himself enough to listen to what the judges had to say. Cheryl Cole was the first to speak. 'Whatever "it" is, you've got it,' she told him, to his delight. 'And I thought your voice was really, really powerful'. Guest judge Natalie Imbruglia agreed, saying Liam was 'impressive, really, really impressive', and adding that other contestants should be 'a little bit worried about you'. Louis Walsh told Liam he was 'really, really glad' he had come back. Three judges in a row had used the words 'really, really' to emphasize their approval of

Liam. However, the judge whose approval he ... 'really, really' wanted was, of course, Simon Cowell.

Walsh handed the conversation over to Cowell, boyishly taunting him with a reminder that 'this is the guy you didn't put through!' Cowell confirmed that Liam 'wasn't quite ready when he came to my house two years ago', and explained how he had advised him to come back two years later. 'I got it right,' said Cowell, never shy of a moment of smugness. Then it was time for the judges to vote 'yes' or 'no'. Given the standing ovation they had given Liam and the gushing comments, there was no doubt about the outcome in viewers' minds. However, for Liam this was still a moment of enormous satisfaction and vindication. Each of the judges' 'yes' votes thrilled him. None more so than Cowell's final verdict: 'Based on talent – absolutely incredible,' he told Liam. 'One massive, fat, almighty yes.' It was an emotional moment for Liam: one could almost see the disappointment of his 2008 rejection lift from his young shoulders.

He then returned backstage where presenter Dermot O'Leary was waiting with the Payne posse. 'You were absolutely tremendous,' Liam's mum told him. O'Leary, who remembered the boy well from 2008, seemed almost as overjoyed and proud as the Paynes. 'The boy becomes a man,' he told Liam, who replied that he felt 'really good' having 'waited two years to get up there and do that'. Liam was so thrilled that he said 'my face hurts' from smiling. In even his wildest dreams, he explained, he had not expected to get such an overwhelmingly positive reaction from the judges. He had exceeded his highest hopes and was through to the next round. 'You know, it was so amazing,' he said. 'Simon stood up for me and that's just the most amazing thing in the world ever.'

In the wake of the audition, he looked back at its true significance. 'It has totally changed my life,' he said. Liam added that had he not re-auditioned, 'I would probably be working in a factory now'. He had still more excitement to come, when he sat down with his family in their Bushbury home to watch his audition broadcast to the nation. 'It was brilliant,' he said. 'My family are so supportive of me and so proud.' When he had left that audition he had vowed to give the next, boot camp, stage of the competition his best go possible. He was ready for the rest of the experience. As we have seen, he used the boot camp phase of the competition in 2008 as a networking opportunity. Little could he know that this time he would not only make four new best friends – but he would end up in a band with them.

Harry auditioned in Manchester. Although he had sung onstage in front of audiences with White Eskimo, this was to be a whole new experience for him: there would be a 3,000-strong live audience, television cameras and, of course, the judges. Even for the placid Harry, a potentially nerve-wracking experience awaited him, but he had plenty of support with him in the form of an entourage of family and friends, each member of which wore a T-shirt bearing the slogan: 'We think Harry has The X Factor!' As for Harry, he was wearing a low-slung white T-shirt with a loose grey cardigan and a green patterned scarf.

'People tell me I'm a good singer,' Harry told host O'Leary. Pointing to Anne, he said: 'It's usually my mum.' O'Leary commented 'And they always say that!', to which Harry readily agreed. 'Singing is what I want to do and if people who can make that happen for me don't think that I should be doing that then that's a major setback in my plans'. He admitted he was 'nervous' as well as 'excited', adding that he felt that only if the judges gave him the thumbs-up would he fully believe he had talent. Lots of friends had praised his voice, but only if the judges did too would he fully believe his friends were not 'lying' in order to make him feel better.

As he waited to go onstage, Harry said the feeling was 'surreal' – the same word Liam had used to sum-up the experience. He was showered with kisses just before he left for the stage, something he found 'a bit embarrassing'. Even O'Leary commented on the awkwardness of the moment, asking: 'Anyone else want to kiss him?' Onstage he appeared confident and comfortable, saying a cheeky 'Hello!' to the judges. But he admitted later that he was 'a right mess' inside. His nerves gave him a huge rush of energy and a natural high. He sang 'Isn't She Lovely' by Stevie Wonder. This is a song he had loved for years and one that he had practised hard in order to perfect his delivery. Unlike most who audition with backing tracks, Harry chose to sing his *a cappella* – without any backing music. He got a good round of applause at the end. Although the reaction was tame in comparison to the near hysteria that had greeted Liam's audition, it was in the scheme of things still a very positive response. Harry took a cheeky, smiling bow in response – a case of mock pride disguising real pride.

He would have cause for even more pride when he heard the verdict of guest Nicole Scherzinger. She told him: 'I'm really glad that we had the opportunity to hear you *a cappella*, cos we could really hear how great your voice is. For sixteen years old, you have a beautiful voice.' Harry, no stranger to the charms of an elegant lady, smiled semi-seductively as he thanked her. Next to speak was Louis Walsh. As the man who guided the careers of boy bands Boyzone and Westlife, his verdict on a young male singer carried a certain amount of extra gravitas. Sadly, although it began on a positive, it included a major rider. 'I agree with Nicole,' said the Irishman. 'However, I think you're so young.

I don't think you have enough experience or confidence yet.' Some members of the audience, which for the most part had really enjoyed Harry's song, were less than impressed with Walsh's verdict, and let him know as much.

Cowell, always up for a chance to tease his old friend Walsh, picked up on that fact as he took his turn to speak. 'Someone in the audience just said "rubbish" and I totally agree with them,' he said. 'Because the show is designed to find someone, whether you're fifteen, sixteen, seventeen – it doesn't matter. I think with a bit of vocal coaching you could actually be very good.' Harry's smile following these comments was adorable – the judges had yet to deliver their final verdicts, but he had already received the sort of vindication he had been hoping for. That said, he wanted to be put through to the next stage, so he anxiously awaited the judging panel's votes.

Walsh, on the left of the panel, spoke first. 'Harry, for all the right reasons I am going to say no,' he said. There was shock, upset and not a little outrage among the audience in response. Cowell encouraged the audience to 'boo' Walsh as loud as they could. As they did so, Harry himself playfully joined in with his own quick 'boo'. A world away from the petulant responses of some who receive a negative on the show, it was a moment of cheeky, playful defiance. In fairness, he could afford to be laid back about it because the other two judges had already given a fair indication they would put him through. Walsh's 'no' vote was indeed quickly overruled by the fact that Cowell and Scherzinger both gave Harry a resounding 'yes'. 'I like you, Harry,' Scherzinger told him, much to Harry's delight. The moment he realized he had got through to boot camp was, he said, one of the best of his life to date. He was through, and as he returned to his family, friends and supporters backstage he found them bubbling over with excitement. Harry was so thrilled he began to be struck by a strange paranoia that somehow the decision would be changed. There was no chance of that happening.

Harry was not the only future member of the band whose initial audition split the panel: the same happened when Niall auditioned in

Dublin. He was living on pure adrenalin on the day as he had been unable to sleep the night before. He knew it was important to get as much sleep as possible ahead of such an important, exciting and potentially draining day, but sleep just would not come. In the end he simply gave up trying and got up to get ready. He wore a checked shirt, blue jeans and trainers. He arrived at the Convention Centre Dublin at the crack of dawn. He was so excited and nervous.

Like Harry, Niall was interviewed on camera prior to his audition. He mentioned that he had been compared to Justin Bieber and added 'it's not a bad comparison'. He said he wanted to sell out arenas, record albums and work with 'some of the best artists in the world'. He said that his audition was the starting point of all that. 'If I get through today – it's game on!' he said, well and truly throwing down the gauntlet. He was coming across as very confident indeed – cocky, almost. But, truth be told, everything that has happened to him since has vindicated that confidence.

As he walked onstage he greeted the crowd with a cheeky 'All right, Dublin?' Then he told Louis Walsh: 'I'm here today to be the best artist

I can be in the world.' His fellow countryman then asked: 'So are you an Irish Justin Bieber?' Niall agreed that he was. After that, he had a bit of banter with guest judge Katy Perry. He was so amazed to find himself jesting with an internationally famous singer such as Perry. Little could he know that within a little over a year he would release his debut album, the title track of which would name-check Perry.

When it came time for him to begin his audition proper, he sang the Jason Mraz hit 'I'm Yours'. Simon Cowell, who had heard so many people audition with this track over recent years, told Niall it was a lazy song to select and asked if he had a second song to perform instead. Niall said he did, and then sang 'So Sick' by Ne-Yo. There was some symbolism to this, as it was one of the songs that Justin Bieber had sung at the Stratford Star talent contest, which, indirectly, made him famous. Niall sang it pleasantly, but slightly un-memorably. His eyes seemed fixed on the back of the venue during the song, in contrast to his future band mates who all directed their attention and energy closer to the judging panel during their respective auditions.

Had he done enough to impress the judging panel? He could not wait to find out. Perry told Niall: 'I think you're adorable! You've got charisma – I just think that maybe you should work on it. You're only sixteen: I started out when I was fifteen and I didn't make it until I was twenty-three.' A slightly mixed verdict, and one that made her final vote hard to predict. Cowell, too, was rather ambiguous. 'I think you're unprepared: I think you came with the wrong song, you're not as good as you thought you were, but I still like you,' he told Niall, who must have been finding it hard to know quite how to take such varied responses.

Could Cheryl Cole offer a more rounded positive critique? The Geordie pop star said: 'Yeah, you're obviously adorable: you've got a lot of charm for a sixteen-year-old, but the song was too big for you, babe.' Everyone seemed to have a 'but' attached to any praise they gave Niall.

The final judge to speak was Louis Walsh. As a fellow Irishman and a man who specializes in managing boy bands, he would be, Niall hoped, more given to appreciate him. 'No, I think you've got something,' Walsh said. 'I think that people will absolutely like you because you're likeable.' In the history of *The X Factor*, that has to rank as one of the more ... eccentric verdicts. Cowell immediately leapt on it, saying, in a sarcastic, withering tone: 'So, people will like him because he's likeable?' The audience burst out laughing and so did Niall. 'Ah, shut up,' snapped Walsh in reply.

When it came to voting time, it was hard to know what each judge would say. It was Cowell who spoke first. 'Well, I'm going to say yes,' he explained. Niall punched the air like a footballer, then kissed his hand and crossed himself. He was quickly deflated when Cole followed with a 'no'. Poor Niall looked absolutely gutted. Perry should have been next to speak but Walsh jumped the queue and told Niall: 'I'm going to say yes!' Contestants need a majority verdict from the panel, meaning that a yes from Perry would be enough to send him through. 'So now,' explained a typically excitable Walsh, 'he needs three yeses!' Perry mimed a stabbing motion into her own neck, signifying how much pressure she now felt under. Cowell, who was sitting observing all of this drama, loved it. Moments of tension such as this are right up his street: he chuckled away at the mischief that Walsh had whipped up.

Perry was less keen on the situation she had been thrust into. Her heart was telling her to put this sweet lad through – but her head was reminding her she had a responsibility to judge with integrity. 'Can I just say that I agree with Cheryl, you do need more experience, and, by the way, just if you're likeable ... likeableness is not going to sell records. It's talent – and you have a seed of it.' She then paused for a moment, prompting Walsh – who by this stage seemed nearly as anxious as Niall – to plead: 'Go ooonnnn!' Perry took one more moment to consider, then said: 'Of course, you're in.' Niall was so thrilled he leapt in the air and began to cheer. As his microphone picked up his cheer it came out surprisingly deep, compared to his singing voice. 'Don't let us down,' Perry warned him as he left the stage. After Niall had gone off, the panel continued to discuss him among themselves. 'He's got charm,' said Cowell. 'He's got something.'

It is moving, with the benefit of hindsight, to re-consider Perry's plea that Niall not let the panel down. He certainly did them proud. After his career with One Direction had made Niall a success in the UK, USA and beyond, Perry Tweeted him, saying: 'Congratulations, you didn't let me down! xo'.

Competitors often describe their experience on *The X Factor* as their 'journey'. Although this has become a horrid cliché – so much so that Cowell even banned the word from being used during one series – in some cases it is literally true. For Zayn, his 'journey' began with ... a long journey. To get from Bradford to his audition he had to set off at two a.m., and to prepare himself for such an early start, he had gone to bed at four o'clock the previous afternoon. His uncle drove him down to Manchester where, like Harry, Zayn auditioned and sang *a cappella*, rather than to a backing track. He had decided to sing the Mario track, 'Let Me Love You'. An R&B classic, this is a song that has been a hit in several countries. He felt nervous as he prepared to walk onto the stage. Once he did so, his nerves worsened. The size of the audience was daunting enough, then he had to get his head around the fact that the ever-frank Simon Cowell was sitting just feet from him.

'My name's Zayn,' he told the panel. He then began to sing 'Let Me Love You'. He had practised hard with this song that he felt confident was perfectly suited to his voice. On the stage he gave it his best go and his rendition was enough to get him through to boot camp. Walsh said that he liked Zayn and Scherzinger said she felt he had something 'special'. Cowell was admiring, too, but added that he felt Zayn needed to become more ambitious. This was a fair criticism at this stage in their relationship. In time, Cowell would appreciate that Zayn's somewhat placid exterior masks a very ambitious soul who wants success and all that comes with it. Indeed, that ambition would not just surface but grow as Zayn continued in the contest. The most immediate hurdle for Zayn came with the voting. Walsh and Scherzinger both said 'yes', and Zayn politely thanked them both. At this stage, with two positive votes, he was already through to boot camp as he had the majority of the three-strong panel in his favour. However, he was naturally keen to complete the set and get the much-prized nod from Cowell. He waited for Cowell to speak with anticipation. 'Zayn, I'm going to say yes,' said the head judge.

Louis Tomlinson was one of the last contestants to audition in the series. There is a certain superstition surrounding the later auditions, as in series one of *Pop Idol*, the eventual winner, Will Young, had been the very last singer to present himself to the judges. Some contestants believe that their chances increase the later in the process they appear. Like Zayn, Louis had needed to leave for the audition at an unseemly hour – in Louis' case he left for Manchester around midnight. His friend Stan went with him. They slept in the car for a while when they arrived at the Manchester MEN Arena and began queuing properly around four a.m. It is significant that contestants are willing to queue for so long and from so early in the morning. Critics of talent shows sometimes complain that fame is 'handed out on a plate' by *The X Factor*.

Yet how many who make this criticism could say that they have ever queued for hours, starting at a ridiculous time, for a job interview? Nobody can take Louis' dedication away from him.

He had quite a different look back on his audition day compared to the one he rocks nowadays. For a start, his hair was much longer. He has since described the lengthy, full-bodied mullet-like look he was sporting that day as 'pretty awful'. Rather than wearing a striped T-shirt as he invariably has in One Direction, he wore a shirt and tie with a baggy grey cardigan and blue jeans. In a sense, Louis' overall audition image fell somewhere between indie cool and boy-going-to-visit-his-granny-to-ask-for-a-cheque. Yet, somehow, it worked.

After sleeping in the queue, only to be rudely awakened by a nudge from a fellow queue member, Louis found himself in the rather coldly named *X Factor* holding room. Time can move slowly in that room. Finally, a member of the production team appeared and called Louis' number. Suddenly, after all the waiting, everything seemed to be happening fast: before he knew it Louis was waiting by the stage. Then, he was told the time had come. As he walked onto the stage he was suddenly a bit scared. As he wrote in the band's official book, his 'mouth went dry'. The way he introduced himself, saying 'My name's Louis Tomlinson', showed how nervous he was. His shy smile said it all, really. Not that his nerves were without advantage: the more shy he comes across the more adorable Louis became in the eyes of many.

The first song he sang was the Scouting For Girls track 'Elvis Ain't Dead', a song that has become typical of the bouncy indie-pop sound of the band. However, before Louis could really get into his stride with the song he was stopped by Cowell, who felt that it would be better if Louis tried another track. For his second track Louis had selected and rehearsed a far tamer song, 'Hey There Delilah' by the Plain White T's. Although this choice would, in months to come, create a problem for Louis, on the day it was enough to win the judges over. Scherzinger showed her approval even during the song, with a big smile on her face as she gently swayed along to the tune.

After Louis sang, Cowell and Walsh both

said his voice was 'interesting' and Scherzinger made a positive comment about his appearance. However, there was a general sense that they felt he was not confident enough. Although Louis has since put this down to his exhaustion on the day, it is undoubtedly true that his confidence came to him later in the competition. Then came the vote and, in common with Niall's experience, it was hard for Louis to know what to expect. His namesake Louis Walsh told him: 'Louis – I'm saying yes'. Scherzinger echoed this, exclaiming: 'I'm saying yes'. Could Louis complete the set with a positive from Cowell? He could. 'You've got three yeses,' said the head judge. Each member of the future band was safely through.

So, what can we learn about the band members from their auditions and their reactions to them? A recurring feature of the boys' recollections is a particularly pronounced desire to win the approval of Simon Cowell. There is nothing so peculiar about this – many *X Factor* contestants admit that it is Cowell's verdict they await most anxiously. However, among the boys there is a sense that they see the head judge as a bit of 'family' figure, and to an extent, Simon Cowell reciprocates. He's not seen as a big brother but more as an 'uncle' figure in the eyes of the band. They would soon name him as such.

Things were looking good for the five boys but there were choppy waters ahead. By the end of the boot camp phase they would have been dumped from the competition, then reinstated as a band. Indeed, it was more of a rollercoaster ride for them. Before the highest of highs the lads would taste the bitterest of lows. 'I met them as solo artists to begin with,' Cowell later told *Rolling Stone* magazine. 'Each of them individually had very good auditions. We had high hopes for two or three of them in particular, and then it all kind of fell apart at one of the latter stages.'

It is worth stating at this point that there's an element of 'legend building' behind the official narrative that has been spun about what happened at boot camp. According to the official narrative, the judges lost faith in each of the boys during the boot camp phase. Only after sending them home, goes the story, did the judges and producers consider that perhaps the boys could be formed into a band. It seems more likely that the decision to form a boy band was taken a little earlier.

The boot camp phase was held at Wembley Arena over five days in July 2010. A total of 211 acts had made it through the auditions to this stage. From the first day of boot camp, on 22 July, it was clear that proceedings would be just as brutal as in past series. Each of the four categories – boys, girls, over-25s and groups – was given a different song to prepare. The boys – including the five future members of One Direction – were given Michael Jackson's 'Man in the Mirror'. This is an all-time pop classic and as such was regarded with reverence by the boys tasked to sing it. (The other categories were also given tricky tracks: the Girls were given 'If I Were a Boy' by Beyoncé; the Groups got 'Nothing's Gonna Stop Us Now' by Starship; while the Over-25s got 'Poker Face', the Lady Gaga hit.)

After the judges had gathered all the contestants, Simon Cowell told them what was at stake on day one of boot camp. 'By the end of the day, half of you are going home,' Cowell told them. 'Today, you're going to be put in your categories and you're going to sing one song. There are literally no second chances today.' No wonder it was such a tense and difficult day. Compared to the opening auditions, during which contestants could sing any song of their choice, they were now feeling constrained creatively and under increasing pressure – which was exactly what the judges and production team wanted them to feel. Boot camp has never been about being fair or friendly: it is a survival-of-the-fittest, edge-of-your-seat ride. Each year there are shocks: some contestants who had looked like finalists or even potential winners in the auditions round suddenly lose their 'mojo' and are eliminated after poor showings. Likewise, some who only just made it through from the auditions suddenly pluck previously unwitnessed talent and charisma out of the bag.

It is not just the contestants that shock – so do the producers. There is often a 'curve ball' surprise thrown in to add drama. In one series, a group of contestants was cut right at the beginning of boot camp. One can only imagine their hurt and disappointment as they realized they were being sent home before they had sung a solitary note, let alone a song. These twists are obviously designed to make dramatic television. For some viewers, though, they make for uncomfortable viewing. To watch people's dreams and emotions being toyed with feels cruel, to say the least.

In 2010, the first twist of boot camp was of a less brutal nature. However, for one future member of One Direction it was still far from within his comfort zone. The five boys were ecstatic when their renditions of 'Man in the Mirror' had been enough to get them through to the second day of the phase. There was much smiling, whooping and cheering back in their hotel rooms that evening. Their confidence and spirits were growing by the day. However, the spirits of one of them came crashing down the following day when the surviving contestants were told that the activity of the day would be not singing – but dancing.

Zayn was not alone in finding this a distinctly uncomfortable and unwelcome brief. Several contestants were unhappy to be dancing. Among them was Irish singer Mary Byrne.

However, nobody reacted quite so extremely as Zayn. Choreographer Brian Friedman told them: 'I don't want you to be scared: what we are going to work on is your stage presence and choreography.' For Zayn, the reassurance came too late. He was crestfallen as he hated dancing: it was when this stage in the series was broadcast that viewers back home would be first introduced to him. He was seen telling a backstage camera: 'I seriously don't want to do it because I hate dancing, and I've never done it before and I feel like an idiot on the stage with other people, who are clearly better than me ... I'm not doing it!' With his discomfort growing, he added: 'When you've got to perform in front of Simon and professionals that know what they're doing and how to dance, and professional choreographers and stuff, and I just don't know ...'

At this stage in the broadcast, Cowell was seen noticing Zayn's absence onstage. In truth, it's more likely that he had been tipped off about the problem by the producers: he has struggled to remember the names of contestants even in the finals of the series, so the idea that he would notice the absence of one contestant on a packed stage seems fanciful. In any case, this made for more drama – the very thing the show thrives on. It also served as a useful way of introducing Zayn, whose initial audition had not been shown on-screen, to the audience. Cowell was shown walking backstage to try and find the absent boy, having told Louis Walsh and Brian Friedman to carry on their work while he found Zayn. When he did so, he asked: 'Zayn, why aren't you out there? You can't just bottle it, you can't just hide behind here! Zayn, you are ruining this for yourself. I'm trying to help you here. So, if you can't do it now, you're never going to be able to do it, right? Come on, let's go and do it!'

So they returned to the stage area. As Zayn was about to hop back onto the stage, Cowell made a final comment, half pep-talk, half warning. 'Don't do that again, get on with it!' he told Zayn. They shook hands – and that was that. The first moment of man management between Cowell and a member of One Direction had occurred. It would not be the last. Once Zayn began dancing it was clear why he had tried to avoid it, and Cowell described his efforts as 'uncomfortable'. For once, the dreaded judge was being charitable rather than cutting. Dancing was clearly not Zayn's strong point. However, the fact that he had been brave enough to give something outside his comfort zone a go will have impressed Cowell and the producers. They would not want to put anyone who buckled under pressure into a band – so although Zayn could not have known it at the time, he had just passed his first test. 'I'm glad that he did it – for himself,' Cowell reflected afterwards. The other four boys had done their best to dance well but none had excelled. Cowell described Niall's efforts, for instance, as 'all over the place'.

The pressure was not going to abate any time soon – and it was not only Zayn who was feeling the pinch. As Harry reflected on-screen, the more hurdles he successfully negotiated, the greater and more intense his ambition became. It was not the case that he was feeling just pleased to be there, or merely proud of what he had achieved thus far. Instead, he was gazing with ever more fiery eyes at what could be achieved. He told the cameras: 'As you go through boot camp you kind of realize how big the prize is, so being here the last few days has made me realize how much I wanna stay – I really don't want to go home now.'

The next twist of the series was one that only indirectly affected our boys but is pertinent to understanding the series they emerged from. Cheryl Cole was sent home after collapsing backstage, and it was later reported that she had contracted malaria while on holiday in Tanzania. She was taken to hospital and told there would be a lengthy recuperation ahead of her. In Cheryl's absence, Cowell called in former Pussycat Dolls singer Nicole Scherzinger to take her place. (Ironically, this made for an unwitting foreshadow of a drama that would erupt on *The X Factor* USA the following year when, after Cole was dropped as a judge, it was Scherzinger who moved from presenter duties to the judges' table.)

As a judge, Nicole Scherzinger was a familiar face to several of the boys as she had been present at the initial auditions of a few of them, including Harry and Louis. With Dannii Minogue also absent, the judging panel was looking quite different to normal. Another change was that the producers decided not to allow an audience to attend the process. The series' official Twitter account sent out the following message: 'Due to the unusual circumstances, we are not inviting an audience to watch the contestants perform at *The X Factor* Boot Camp.' This handed an added dose of drama to what happened next.

On the third day of boot camp the contestants were handed a list of forty songs from which to choose one to sing. For some this was a gift: unlike day one when they felt restricted, they now felt liberated. For others, though, this made life tougher: they simply could not decide which of the songs they most wanted to sing. As soon as they decided on one, they would notice another track in the list that also appealed. When they could have been working hard on perfecting their chosen track they were instead prevaricating. This was the final hurdle before judges' houses – a terrible time to be unfocused. Once it came to their time to sing they would take to the stage individually, perform, and then leave. The judges would not be giving them any feedback at the time of the performance.

Liam has chosen to sing 'Stop Crying Your Eyes Out' by Oasis. It was not a difficult choice for him. As we have seen, he loves Oasis and had sung their songs since he was a little kid, adopting the famous Liam Gallagher posture. Before he went on stage, he explained on camera what was at stake for him. He described his successful first audition as 'a brilliant bonus – my feet still haven't touched the floor'. He then said that there was also 'a negative' about it: 'because I've got to try and live back up to it'. Having had a year to prepare for his opening audition he had just twenty-four hours to get ready for his next one. He was shown making a mistake during rehearsals, and Brian Friedman said that this was due to 'his age'. Again, for Liam the moment was to be all about pleasing Cowell. 'I want to prove to Simon that I'm here and I mean business,' he said. 'I want to show him that I've got what it takes.'

He walked onstage with grace and confidence. 'Hi everybody. How are you doing, judges?' he asked, casually. Before singing, he was invited to explain why he felt he had the 'x factor'. With his right leg shuffling with nerves, Liam said he felt he had it, 'because I had a knock-back at an early age – I took on a huge challenge, set myself a goal and I never gave up'. As in past appearances in front of Cowell, Liam had pitched himself well.

Then he sang the Oasis song. This was a performance that divided viewers: some felt it was a bit stale and boring, many felt it was an emotional and convincing rendition. Certainly, it lacked some of the drama of his 'Cry Me a River' audition, but as Liam had noted, that was always going to be a tough one to live up to, not least due to the absence of a huge live audience this time. Indeed, Liam was beginning to inject some more oomph into it when Cowell cut him off. With that, it was time for him to leave and let the judges discuss his prospects without him present. 'Oh, Simon, he's good,' whispered Walsh after Liam had left the stage. 'I like him. Simon, girls are going to like him,' added the Irishman. Cowell's body language showed he was not convinced. 'I like him, but I think he's a little bit one dimensional,' he said. Walsh continued to put Liam's case. 'He's a young pub singer, Simon,' he said. 'And he's only sixteen.'

Later, Cowell showed that he was less than convinced. Speaking on the sister show *The*

Xtra Factor, he said: 'The world we live in today, compared to a year ago, is that you have to stand out from the rest. So someone like Liam is an example of who, maybe a year or two years ago, I would have thought of as a good contestant on this show. But now he just bores the pants off me.' Expanding on his theme, he said: 'When there's a ceiling on somebody's talent, which there is with Liam, you can only take him so far, so you're always limited by that. When you're working with someone that's frustrating, because you want to feel that you can throw anything at them and they'll cope with it or make it better.' None of this painted a rosy future for Liam.

Once he and the other four boys – whose day three songs were not broadcast – had performed, it was time for the judges to confer. Due to the continued absence of Minogue and Cole, a few changes were made to the format. Instead of putting six acts through in each category, Cowell, Walsh and Scherzinger agreed to send eight acts to each judges' house. This partly reflected their confidence that there were many acts worthy of progression and partly to allow Minogue and Cole the chance to have a

121

wider crop of acts to choose from. A change was also made to the category age divisions. At Scherzinger's suggestion the over-25s were changed to the over-28s.

When the thirty remaining boys – including Harry, Liam, Louis, Niall and Zayn – were called to the stage, they could hardly have been more anxious. Zayn arrived nervously rubbing his hands together. Liam looked like he wanted to faint – or cry. Then the judges began to announce the names of those who had got through. Cowell started by naming John Wilding, then Scherzinger announced Nicolo Festa's name. As more and more names were announced, the boys became more nervous and scared. It was notable, though, that Louis made a point of clapping and smiling politely to acknowledge the joy of each contestant who had been lucky enough to have their name announced. He even patted Karl Brown on the back as he got the nod. His grace made the knowledge of the disappointment he was feeling all the more heart-breaking for the onlooker.

Eventually, there was just time for two more names to be announced. Each of the five boys hoped that his would be one of them, while also despairing that this was not going to be the case. The final two names called out were those of Matt Cardle, the eventual winner, and Tom Richards. 'That's it, guys – I'm really sorry,' said Cowell. As Richards left the stage in tears of joy, the contestants remaining onstage tried to come to terms with the fact that they were out. Liam, who had been rejected at this stage in 2008 only to be reinstated minutes later, shuffled uncomfortably from foot to foot as he faced the reality of elimination. He held his hand to his head and fought tears. The tears won the battle. Harry looked out in shock and Niall ruffled his own hair, a look of desperation and heartbreak etched into his face.

When Liam left the stage he was given a commiserating hug by Dermot O'Leary. 'I just don't want to go home,' he said, barely audibly. 'I just don't want to go.' Then Harry spoke. Though he seemed to be handling it marginally better than Liam he was, he explained, 'really gutted' and he looked it. Niall, meanwhile, was more animated. With him a sense of anger seemed present amid his heartbreak. 'Worst thing I've ever felt in my life,' he said. 'Standing there, waiting for your name to be called, and then it's not.' As tears returned to his eyes he apologized to the interviewer and walked away, covering his face with his jumper.

However, Cowell was not happy to lose the boys. 'I had a bad feeling that maybe we shouldn't have lost them and maybe there was something else we should do with them,' he explained later in an interview with *Rolling Stone*. 'And this is when the idea came about that we should see if they could work as a group.' Whether the decision was made on the spur of that moment or whether it had been a more premeditated option, it was now time to act on it. A boy band and a girl band – to be named Belle Amie – would be formed out of some of the rejected contestants. Backstage, the production team gathered Louis, Liam, Harry, Niall and Zayn together. They also called back the four girls, who would be formed into Belle Amie.

At this stage none of them knew what was in store. For Liam, this was a particularly surreal moment. Just as in 2008, he had been told he was going home only to be recalled minutes later. As they were led back to the stage more than one of the boys and girls were anxiously biting their fingernails. The boys lined up on the stage. Their faces and body language said it all: they were downcast to have been rejected by the competition, confused as to why they had been called back, and were simultaneously trying to keep a lid on their expectations. Meanwhile, the judges looked at the two groups and wondered silently to themselves whether they had made the right decision. As Cowell looked at the five boys, he had no doubt. 'The minute they stood there for the first time together – it was a weird feeling,' he told *Rolling Stone* later. 'They just looked like a group at that point.' They did indeed. There is something touching, almost eerie, about the way the five boys melded into a single unit in that moment.

It was Scherzinger who kicked-off the explanation. 'Hello, thank you so much for coming back,' she told them. 'Judging from some of your faces, this is really hard. We've thought long and hard about it and we've thought of each of you as individuals and we just feel that you're too talented to let go of. We think it would be a great idea to have two separate groups.' Still, the penny had not completely dropped with the contestants, so Cowell decided to make it clear. 'We've decided to put you both through to the judges' houses,' he told them. The five boys erupted with joy – Louis leapt like a kangaroo, while Harry sank to his knees. The judges looked on with happiness as they witnessed the relief and excitement. Then Cowell decided it was time to give them a reality check. 'Guys, guys, girls, girls – this is a lifeline: you've got to work ten, twelve, fourteen hours a day, every single day, and take this opportunity,' he told them. 'You've got a real shot here, guys.'

The lads bounced off the stage feeling like they had just won the FA Cup. Harry spoke for all five when he told O'Leary: 'I went from the worst feeling in my life to the best.' Then it was time for them to be reunited with the other contestants who had made it through earlier. They ran into each other's arms and embraced. Life felt really good. However, there was to be one more barrier for the boys to negotiate. They were asked to make absolutely sure that they were happy to be formed into a band.

After all, each had auditioned very much as a solo artist. Nobody wanted a band containing a member whose heart was not in the idea of performing as a unit, so it was a sensible decision to encourage each boy to search their souls. It was Liam who took time to make up his mind. Since his 2008 *X Factor* experience he had worked hard to build the beginnings of a solo career. At first, he felt it was unimaginable to leave all that work behind and instead join a band. He searched his soul, took advice from those he respected and trusted most, and then came to a clear decision: he was in. It was in that very moment that the band was officially formed.

The next milestone came when the judges were informed which category they would be mentoring for the remainder of the series. The production team telephoned each judge with the news, and Simon Cowell was told he would be given the groups. Traditionally, the groups are seen as one of the two weaker categories – along with the elder solo category. Although he knew that One Direction were a strong prospect, Cowell played up to the script by sarcastically responding to the news, saying: 'Thank you for repaying all of my hard work on the show this year.' As this episode was broadcast, *X Factor* viewers lapped up the drama surrounding the formation of One Direction and Belle Amie. Among the viewers were the band members and their families. Louis' mother, Johannah, told the local press: 'We had a family party to watch the boot camp stages of the show on Sunday and we were all so proud of Louis and the boys. He's so excited, he can't quite believe he has made it this far.'

For the judges' houses phase of the show, the band flew to Marbella in Spain to perform in front of Cowell. For the successful acts in this stage of the process the prize is huge: a place in the live shows. For the unsuccessful acts, the disappointment is just as strong. As Liam knew, and any footballer will tell you, losing a semi-final is worse than losing a final. For *X Factor* contestants much the same is true of the judges' houses, which is, in effect, the semi-final stage. The boys were nervous and excited – Zayn particularly so as this was his first trip abroad.

(*From top, left to right*)
Five solo acts Niall,
Harry, Louis, Liam and
Zayn become a band:
One Direction is born.

Above: Dazzled by fans: posing with mentor Simon Cowell who would lead the boys to the final.

Below: Which one's which? You can bet all their fans know.

Above: Born to do it: the boys strike a cheeky pose on the red carpet at the premiere of *The Chronicles of Narnia: The Voyage of the Dawn Treader*.

Below: With fellow contestants of series seven, including eventual winner Matt Cardle.

Left: The band becomes the face of Pokémon.

Below: Starting out with a bang: their debut single 'What Makes You Beautiful' tops the UK charts.

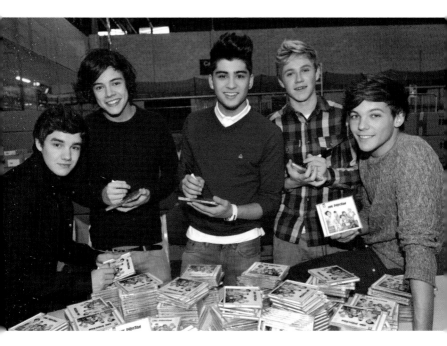

Above: The band launch *Up All Night* – the fastest-selling album of 2011.

Below: Ecstatic as they cradle their award for Best British Single.

The only way is up: One Direction on the Up All Night tour that began in December 2011 and took in Europe, Australasia and North America.

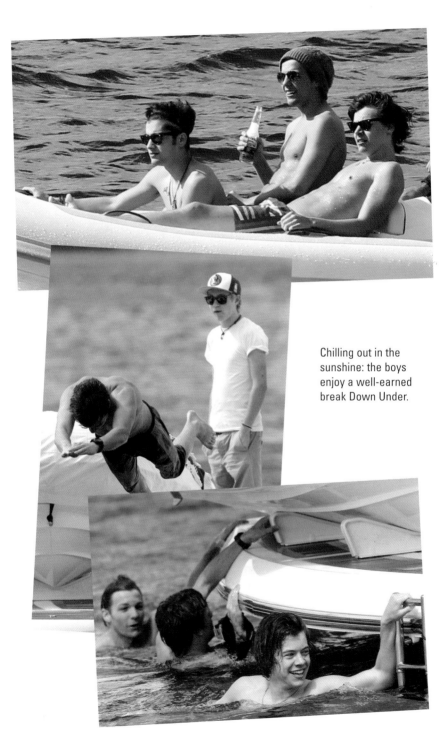

Chilling out in the sunshine: the boys enjoy a well-earned break Down Under.

Above: Conquering the States: One Direction became the first British group to reach number one on the US *Billboard* chart with their debut album.

Below: From talent-show contestants to global stars: there's only One Direction.

He had needed to apply for a passport especially for the trip. Boys will be boys, so there were some fun moments in Marbella – though the tabloid reports of Cowell's house being trashed were rather colourfully exaggerated. However, they did have time to sit by the beach. Louis and Zayn fondly remember sitting together eating pizza, looking out into the sea.

However, they were there to work and were determined to succeed. They would do so in some style. They did not so much convince Cowell of their talent, as blow him away. Speaking later to *Rolling Stone* magazine about the band's history, Cowell was asked when he first realized that the band could be huge. 'When they came to my house in Spain and performed, after about a millionth of a second,' he said. 'I tried to keep a straight face for a bit of drama for the show.'

For their performance, the boys sang 'Torn', originally a hit for Australian singer Natalie Imbruglia, who had been a guest judge at Liam's audition earlier in the series. But there was drama before the audition when Louis was stung by a sea urchin while the boys frolicked in the ocean. At first he assumed he had cut his foot on a sharp stone or piece of glass. However, when he woke the next morning he was horrified to discover that his foot had swollen to twice its normal size. When he got up to deal with this he fell over. He called for help and was taken to hospital, where he was given an injection. The shock of the pain from the needle was so intense that poor Louis reportedly threw up.

Meanwhile, the rest of the band waited anxiously to see if he would be able to perform. When they saw him arrive back from hospital they were so thrilled they ran to smother him in hugs and then lifted him between them and chaired him along to their showdown performance. Cowell quickly noticed Louis' slight limp when they arrived to sing. Louis assured the judge that he was fine. Then they sang. Liam led the vocals during the first verse, Harry took the bridge and then all five sang during the chorus. As they swung their hips during the final chorus, the band suddenly looked surprisingly convincing as a unit, considering the tender age of both the band itself and its individuals.

At the end of the song Cowell gave nothing away to the band, merely saying: 'See you later'. However, as the boys filed away from the audition, Cowell was struggling to contain his enthusiasm. He and his aide Sinitta both expressed their excitement over what they had seen. 'The second they left I jumped out of my chair,' he recalled in *Rolling Stone*. 'They just had it. They had this confidence. They were fun. They worked out the arrangements themselves. They were like a gang of friends, and kind of fearless as well.' There would be little soul-searching needed when he decided whether to put One Direction through to the live shows.

Still, when it came to breaking the news to them the following day, Cowell naturally played it as deadpan as he could while building theirs and the viewers' suspense. 'My head is saying it's a risk and my heart is saying that you deserve a shot,' he told them. The boys stood waiting, practically breathless with anxiety. Liam was particularly tense – he did not want to go home at this stage for the second time running. 'And that's why it's been difficult. So I've made a decision. Guys, I've gone with my heart – you're through!'

The roar that came from the boys as they

celebrated said it all. They then ran to celebrate with Cowell – Harry the first to arrive in the arms of their mentor. 'I am so impressed with all of you, I mean that,' Cowell told them. Four of the newly confirmed finalists then jumped fully clothed into the nearby swimming pool. 'We went crazy,' remembered Liam. Louis, still under the weather from the sting, decided not to join them in the water.

On the plane home to England the band members were in jubilant mood. They had made it through to the live shows and would soon be singing live in front of the nation. It was, to use the phrase bawled out at the start of each *X Factor* live show, time … to face … the music!

7 GOING LIVE!

In truth, the most fearsome thing that contestants face in the live shows is not 'the music', or even the judges. Instead, it is the public vote. The live shows are an exciting experience for all acts. Not only do they perform to a live studio audience and a primetime TV audience of millions, they also face weekly feedback from each of the four judges. Having successfully dealt with all of that they then face the public vote. The phone lines are closed after twenty-four hours and the bottom two acts then face a 'sing-off', before the judges decide which of the two will be sent home. As they prepared for the first weekend, the boys were just hoping to make it through to week two. Little could they know then that they had ten weeks of live shows ahead of them, as they would make it all the way to the grand final.

Each week the judges would be offering their opinions on them. Although the feedback was mostly positive, each judge had their individual quirks, with which the boys would become more familiar as time went on. For instance, Louis Walsh habitually deemed them 'the next big boy band'. His laudatory thoughts were tinged only by a tendency to banter with Simon Cowell at their expense. Dannii Minogue, though, was the most critical on the panel. She was never harsh and her observations were fair, accurate and aimed at getting the best out of the band. She was the most frank and the least caught-up with One Direction mania. Cheryl Cole, meanwhile, made amusing admissions of a growing One Direction fandom. Cowell was his usual confident self. As the band's mentor, not to mention the king of the *X Factor* universe, he sat with broad shoulders – both literally and metaphorically – as his young prodigies sailed through, week by week. Let's start at the beginning ...

Week One
Theme: Number ones

In the first week, the band sang 'Viva La Vida' by Coldplay. It was a song choice that took many viewers by surprise. As such, a bold statement was being made early on: this was not going to be yet another unimaginative boy band. It might have been tempting to hand them a crooning Westlife ballad, a Take That anthem or a romp by The Wanted. Yet instead, they were given a Coldplay song. 'You wouldn't actually connect this band normally with this song – but strangely, it works,' said Cowell, during the introductory VT, the brief, personalized video that is aired immediately prior to each contestant's performance. Zayn explained he was worried he might miss his cue. He felt quite overwhelmed by the length and intensity of the build-up to the first live show.

As the drama of the VT built, Cole said: 'These guys really need to step up and deliver – there's a lot of pressure!' The band stood waiting for the doors at the back of the stage to open. Beyond those doors were the studio audience, judges and the cameras that would transport them into the living rooms of millions. Harry was so nervous he had been sick. However, the band had, Louis explained, made sure they focused on their own song, rather than worrying about the opposition. It was a wise approach, and now came the time to deliver.

As the band appeared and sang the song, each boy showed a different emotion. Liam, at the centre of it all, looked masterful and poised. His superior experience of live performance and of television was clear. Late in the song when the performance wilted slightly, it was Liam who burst into action – urging the other band members to up their games. Harry, meanwhile, showed his nerves with an intense, almost aggressive stage presence. As he thumped his shoulder to the beat his facial expression tried, unsuccessfully, to conceal his nerves. Zayn, as had been anticipated, did look concerned in the seconds before his cue, but after successfully meeting it he began to look happier and get into his stride.

Which leaves us with Louis and Niall. Mr Tomlinson looked simply delighted to be there, more or less relaxed onstage and with his usual sense of fun. Perhaps the combination of his being the eldest member of the group and his comparatively lesser responsibilities during the song combined to create his sense of comfort. Niall, meanwhile, managed to smile the whole way through the performance. Rarely has anyone looked happier to be in a band. His smile showed itself not just through his lips but in his eyes too, which shone with joy. Even as he sang his part, the lyrics dealing with regret and disappointment, he continued to smile. The incongruity of this was forgivable in the circumstances – it was just nice to see someone enjoying himself so much.

As the band moved into position for Liam's solo, concluding line, they were already smiling with excitement, satisfaction and not a little relief that they had got through the song so well. At the end, they embraced each other, not unlike a group of boys in the park at the end of a football match. It was these moments that reminded viewers what they were watching: a band of schoolboys at the very, very start of their career. This made them all the more impressive and enchanting because it leant them an 'underdog' identity – all the better to attract the public vote.

The panel applauded, and Cowell smiled with avuncular pride. Louis told them: 'Wow guys, when I heard you were going to do Coldplay I thought it was a big, big risk! I love what you did with the song – you totally made it your own. I love that the band is gelling, even though Simon's going to claim he put this band together: it was my idea originally, Simon. It was! Boys, I think potentially you could be the next big boy band, but you have a lot of work to do.' He added, with a sting: 'But Simon Cowell, I'm not sure about the styling! Did you have a stylist?' As the audience indulged in some pantomime booing, Walsh hardened his face and jutted out his chin.

Dannii Minogue then spoke. 'Guys, I don't know whose idea it was because I wasn't there, but you look like you fit together, you're the perfect band,' she said. The boys were so thrilled with the feedback they congratulated one another. Their enthusiasm was infectious. 'That song was fantastic and you did make it your own,' added the Australian. Cheryl Cole felt the same way. 'I have to agree with Dannii, you look like you were meant to be together as a group,' she said, to the continued delight of One Direction. 'I reckon the girls will be going crazy for you, but you need a little bit more time to develop as a group, that's all. Just a little bit more time.'

Their mentor then chipped in. 'Regarding your role in putting the group together, Louis, we'll rewind the tapes on that one,' said Cowell. Walsh defiantly told him he should. 'You guys came together because your boot camp auditions weren't good enough but you were too good to throw away,' Cowell continued. 'We took a risk, and I've got to tell you, what was so impressive about that was when you started to screw up: one of you at the end, Liam stepped in, you brought it back together. That's what bands do.' He then turned to Walsh's comments regarding styling: 'Louis, I don't want to style a band like this. We asked the band to do whatever they wanted to do – I'm not going to interfere, they're going to do it their way. It was brilliant, guys.'

Onstage, Dermot O'Leary joined the conversation, saying: 'Louis, with the greatest respect, how do you know what eighteen-year-olds should be wearing? Come on, man!' Harry stood aside from all the squabbling and summed up what the band was thinking: 'It was the best experience of all of our lives,' he said. Zayn later reflected that each band member was 'buzzing' as they left the stage. They had each just had their biggest-ever dose of 'performance high'.

The following evening they nervously awaited their fate as the public vote was announced. After the series had ended, Liam said that waiting for the results of the first week's public vote was the one that made them most nervous. They survived the vote to go through to week two. Less lucky was Nicolo Festa, who left automatically after finishing bottom, and FYD, who lost the sing-off with Katie Waissel.

Meanwhile, Cowell had noticed something very special about One Direction – they were quickly attracting huge gatherings of fans outside the studio. 'It was unusual because, in an instant, we had hundreds of fans outside the studio,' he would later tell *Rolling Stone*. 'That doesn't happen very often.' Expanding on the exchange he had with Walsh over the band's styling, he explained: 'They had good taste and they understood the kind of group they wanted to be. They didn't want to be moulded. I'm not interested in working with people like that either.'

The early signs were all rather positive.

Week Two
Theme: Heroes

In the second week of the live shows, fourteen acts still remained. This figure was itself a reminder to One Direction and their fellow contestants of the scale of the challenge: even having shed two acts in week one, there were still thirteen other acts to see the back of before a winner would be crowned. They would all have to work hard. It was a tough week for the band because Harry had another attack of nerves during the sound check. He could not breathe properly and felt like he was going to be sick again. It is remarkable to reflect that

Harry, who is now the central and oftentimes effortlessly confident figure of the band, was the one who struggled most with the pressure early on. It was a surprise to him, too, as he had never before been so hit by nerves that his ability to perform was called into question.

Their song for the week was 'My Life Would Suck Without You', by Kelly Clarkson. There was a nice symbolism behind the song choice: Clarkson, who won the first ever series of *American Idol*, is one of the most successful graduates of television talent show history. However, musically, as a female solo artist's song, it was again an unlikely choice. The band performed it well. They were moodily lit for the opening section. As Liam took the opening verse the camera panned between the others. It immediately showed Niall and Louis grinning again, while Harry was again jutting along to the music. Zayn? He was looking broody and sultry. By the end of the song the relief and joy of all members was palpable. So Zayn might have delivered one less than perfect note – the important thing was that they had basically nailed it. Louis offered the nervous Harry a protective hug.

Walsh, as is customary in feedback to acts that he is not mentoring, was the first to speak. 'Well, One Direction, you seem to be having fun on stage,' he said. 'Every schoolgirl up and down the country is going to love this. My only problem, boys, is with your mentor, Simon. Kelly Clarkson a hero? Simon, why? It was a strange song. Boys, you are really, really good but I think Simon Cowell could've picked a better song.' As the pantomime boos rang out, Dannii Minogue said: 'Boys, maybe that's your musical hero. I have to say that you're five heartthrobs. You look great together and Harry, whatever nerves you have, I'm sure your friends and you will stick together. The true measure of a boy band like you will be when you sing your big ballad, so I will be looking forward to hearing that.' The band appreciated her feedback – not least because they were themselves dying to sing a ballad.

'I can't even cope with how cute you are. Seriously, I can't!' said Cheryl Cole. Harry put his hands together in a praying motion, his prayers had just been answered. 'I just want to go over and hug them, in a nice way. You're so sweet, I'm watching you the whole time just thinking, "This is adorable!".' All the while, Cowell comically warned her off the boys, saying: 'No ... no ... no!' When it came to his time to judge, he offered the band some colossal praise. 'Let me tell you, you are the most exciting pop band in the country today,' he told the boys, much to their shock and awe. Liam in particular looked stunned by the statement. 'I'm being serious – there is something absolutely right.' Cowell has never been one to measure his remarks: acts tend to be the best or worst he has ever seen. Nobody in the studio was letting that get in the way of their excitement, though. As the audience cheered Cowell's words, Harry theatrically urged them to cheer louder. There was even louder cheering and celebrations galore when One Direction were again sent through by the public vote.

Week Three
Theme: Guilty pleasures

They recounted the crazy experience they and the other remaining finalists had enjoyed and endured during a high-profile shopping outing to Topshop on Oxford Street in the build up to week three. It was their first proper encounter with the hysteria that was growing among their increasing fan base. As they arrived, the screams from the girls were deafening. In years to come this would seem a small-fry encounter for the band, but at the time it was almost terrifyingly intense. 'He winked at me, he winked at me, he winked at me!' screamed one of the girls, convinced she had 'had a moment' with one of the band. Louis recounted how they were 'absolutely mobbed by teenage girls, which is all right!' So, too, were the free clothes they were allowed to pick up during the trip. Simon Cowell's close relationship with Topshop owner Sir Philip Green was responsible for this outing being a feature of the series.

Returning to the music, Cowell explained how during the week he had changed the song that the band would sing. As ever with *The X Factor*, such an unremarkable decision was hyped and dramatized into an obstacle of almost cinematic consequence. Having presented this as a challenge that, in the words of Dannii Minogue, many acts would not be able to overcome, the band were given that invaluable identity for a talent show: the underdog.

The new song was 'Nobody Knows' by Pink. With a slightly more sombre tune the band – even Louis and Niall – looked more serious and soulful than in previous weeks. Here was the closest One Direction had come to that boy band standard: the ballad. At the climax of the song the producers even deployed pyrotechnics behind them. Louis could not resist turning for a look at them as they went off.

Perhaps the more significant aspect of this performance was that Harry sang alone in parts. While Liam was still very much the lead member, Harry's confidence was rising and, with it, so too was his place in the One Direction pecking order. Walsh paid tribute to Liam's lead in his feedback. 'You just have to walk out on the stage: everybody's screaming,' said the Irishman.

'It's like five Justin Biebers! And Liam – brilliant lead vocal from you!' Minogue observed that they were 'living the dream'. Cole, though, stole the night with her comment, which had the audience and band enraptured. 'You know what, guys?' she asked, 'Let me just put this out there: you are my guilty pleasure!' Praise from the gorgeous Cole: that was, right there, irrefutable evidence that the band were indeed living the dream. Cole added: 'Whenever The Beatles went anywhere, they caused that level of hysteria. You're finding your feet now, I'm looking forward to seeing you improve even more.'

Cowell was his usual proud self. Having milked the whole song change issue for all he could, he said: 'I've got to tell you, apart from it being a great performance, I thought vocally, you've really, really made some really huge improvements.' Backstage after they had performed, Harry spoke with excitement about another week of praise from the judges. 'The comments were absolutely brilliant,' he beamed. 'For us to keep proceeding in the competition, we have to get better every week.'

In keeping with the spirit of the week, the band were asked what their own top three choices would be as guilty pleasure songs. Having been named by Cole as her choice, they in turn revealed that their ultimate guilty pleasure track was, they said, John Travolta singing 'Greased Lightning'. Behind that was 'Tease Me' by Chaka Demus & Pliers and in third place was that infuriatingly catching, cheesy pop hit 'I'm Too Sexy' by Right Said Fred.

For their growing fan base One Direction were not a guilty but a proud pleasure. Girls across the country were screaming from the rooftops of their love for the new boy band. As for the lads themselves, they sailed into week three after the public vote was announced. They had seen judge Cole perform live during the weekend shows. The sort of iconic fame she enjoyed was just what they had wanted from the day they first applied to the show. Now, having survived the dreaded bottom two for two successive weeks, their confidence was really growing. Though they tried to keep their feet on the ground, they began to dare to believe. It was game on.

Week Four
Theme: Halloween

The themes for the live shows of *The X Factor* are sometimes rather unimaginative, but for the third week of the series the 'Halloween' theme promised more fun than usual. During the intervening week the contestants had visited the London Dungeon and Niall, in particular, was quite freaked out by the experience. On Saturday night, with songs such as Michael Jackson's 'Thriller', 'Bat Out of Hell' by Meatloaf and 'Bewitched' by Steve Lawrence among the songs the acts sang, and with scary sets including vampires, witches and the like, it made for a ghoulish evening. One Direction sang the Bonnie Tyler hit 'Total Eclipse of the Heart'. Having been covered by Westlife, this was a song more in keeping with a boy band.

Done up in ghostly, vampiric make-up, the boys looked the part on a stage laced with dry ice. Although Harry stood in the centre of the line-up, it was Liam who again led the vocals. Niall popped in with some backing lines, and Zayn leant his suitably smoky voice too. The audience's applause at the end of the song was notably louder and longer than for any of the other acts that evening. As they listened to the acclaim the band stood with more pride and comfort than before.

'I love the whole *Twilight*, vampire thing going on in the background,' said Walsh, leading the judges' feedback. 'Simon, it's definitely working.' The absence of Walsh's tendency to tease Cowell about his act showed how they had become more of a prospect. Minogue added: 'You make vampire hot – I want to come to your party!' As for Cole, she too spoke with excitement at the band's commercial potential: 'It doesn't matter where I go, somebody, an older woman, young women, kids ... everybody mentions One Direction. I think you have a really long way to go in this competition.'

It was left to their proud mentor to sum up the band's performance. 'What I really admire about you guys,' began Cowell, 'is I know people are under pressure when you go into a competition like this. You've got to remember you're sixteen, seventeen years old. The way you've conducted yourselves: don't believe the hype ... work hard, rehearse. Honestly, it's a total pleasure working with you lot.' Dermot O'Leary summed-up the atmosphere when he said, simply: 'Wow!' On the following night's show, Harry said: 'Last night felt brilliant. We got a real chance to show off our vocals and hopefully the fans at home will vote and keep us in because we really don't want to go home now.'

The fans at home did vote. The band was through to fight another week.

Week Five
Theme: American Anthems

If there was a week in which One Direction truly stamped their authority on the competition it was in week five. They were given the final slot – the dream slot – on the night, much prized because it means you perform just minutes before the lines open for the public to vote. With your, hopefully, climactic, performance fresh in the viewers' minds, you have a good chance of attracting high voting numbers. 'You know what they say about saving the best till last,' said Cowell, introducing them with that smile of his that combines a touch of pride with a dash of cheek and a large helping of smug. It was clear Cowell believed there was something special to come.

There certainly was. Following an introductory VT that showed the boys messing around in the contestants' house – including some gratuitous scenes of Harry and Zayn in just their underwear – they appeared on the stage to sing the Kim Wilde hit, 'Kids in America'. Wearing colourful outfits, including classic American baseball jackets, and with cheerleader girls behind them, the boys did indeed look like a band from the other side of the Atlantic. They would have looked quite in place on a Disney television series, or even *High School Musical*. They moved off the stage at one point, singing on the raised platform behind the judges, taking them just inches from the screaming audience.

It was a performance of great authority. The way Harry leapt up at the end of the song, landing with a defiant thump on the final note, summed up their confidence. Walsh told the band how far they had already come. 'Listen, everywhere

I go there's hysteria, it's building on this band,' he said. 'You remind me a bit of Westlife, Take That, Boyzone ... you could be the next big band.' Minogue stepped out of the aforementioned hysteria to offer a more considered judgement. 'I don't think, vocally, it was the best of the night but a great performance,' she said. Cole told One Direction: 'That absolutely cheered me up and brightened up my night, I thoroughly enjoyed that performance. You are great kids: I love chatting to you backstage, you are just good lads, nice lads.' Then proud old Uncle Simon declared: 'That was without question your best performance by a mile.'

The future suddenly looked bright, though a shadow was cast over it when some viewers accused the band of miming during their rendition of the Kim Wilde track. They pointed out that at one point in the song Zayn looked as if he had missed his cue, yet his voice was audible before he lifted the microphone to his mouth. Twitter quickly surged with accusations that the band was miming. In due course, former *X Factor* winner Shayne Ward was quoted in the *Sun* newspaper, attacking the band for miming.

This controversy was not what the band wanted to be reading. It only seemed yesterday that they had been five ordinary teenage boys. Now, they were facing their first 'media storm'. Their defence was that while Zayn did miss his cue, it was not his voice that could be heard but Harry's. With the camera focusing on Zayn, it was easy for viewers to miss this fact. This partially placated their online critics. Ward quickly distanced himself from the miming allegations, saying the journalist had twisted his words.

When the results were announced on the Sunday evening show the band was relieved to learn that they had once again survived the public vote. The miming controversy got them down at the time, but it also offered them a valuable lesson in the realities of fame and success. They realized that, while they had a huge, dedicated and growing fan base, they also faced non-stop scrutiny from those who were less enamoured of them. The live shows were proving to be a crash-course in fame for One Direction.

Week Six
Theme: Elton John

Elton John's music is, obviously, composed with a solo performer in mind. As the last band standing in the series, One Direction had to choose carefully which song they would pick from his vast and stately back catalogue. They went with 'Something About the Way You Look Tonight'. They had the penultimate slot on the night. Harry, standing in the centre of the line-up, contributed his most significant solo of the series to date. The show's producers had noted the growing frenzy around him and, with his poise growing week by week, were moving him to a more leading role in the band. As he began his first line, the screams and howls from the audience showed this was a popular move.

Cowell gave the band a standing ovation at the end and, throughout his fellow judges' commentary, whipped up the audience to cheer louder. Walsh told the lads: 'Well, boys, after that performance I think you're only going in one direction, and that direction is the final. I talked to you guys a lot yesterday and I really got to know you. I know that you're taking the whole thing really, really serious and you know, you're going to be the next big boy band.' Dannii Minogue added: 'Guys, you are so consistent, it's scary!' Cheryl Cole, hearing the huge and frenzied cheer from the studio audience, said: 'Listen to that! That's what it's all about; to hear that is the measure of what you've become.'

Finally, Simon Cowell said: 'Guys, I want to say something, okay? This is the first time in all the years of *X Factor* where I genuinely believe a group are going to win this competition.' He then reflected on their courteous and professional personalities, before concluding: 'Guys, congratulations'.

Everything was rosy in the world of One Direction. The series had taken a gamble by forming the band in front of the viewers' eyes, yet it was a gamble that was paying off. Each week their stature and popularity was growing. Louis, talking about their Elton evening, said: 'Last night was absolutely incredible, the crowd were amazing.' Zayn sounded a more cautious note. Assessing how the challenge was adapting week by week, he reflected that, 'The competition's really, really heating up.' It really was – and the growing One Direction army felt that the hottest act of the lot was the band.

Week Seven
Theme: The Beatles

At last: a genre that fitted a boy band best! Surrounded by male and female solo artists, One Direction had endured weekly themes that were not really in the comfort zone of a band. However, The Beatles week was right up their street. This was particularly true of Liam, who told the official *X Factor* website: 'I'm a massive fan of The Beatles and I'm really looking forward to tonight.' He previewed a 'complicated performance', which would be 'full of harmonies and ad libs, but it's the sort of performance that I think you'd expect from a top boy band.'

They sang an up tempo version of 'All You Need is Love'. Harry again took plenty of the vocals, and what had started as a quiet performance ended in rapture, with dancers behind the band bouncing up and down. It was not, though, without its imperfections. 'Thank God for you guys,' said Walsh in his feedback, adding that, 'it is good to see the Fab Five singing the Fab Four'. Minogue, though, sounded a note of criticism. 'I've always given you good comments,' she began, 'I just have to say tonight, you guys [Zayn and Niall], were struggling. I don't know if it was caught on-camera, but you were struggling with the backing vocals. Don't let the other guys down, you have to work as a group.' Cowell, when it came to his turn, spoke in competitive tones. Gesturing to his three fellow judges, he said: 'This lot do not want you to do well in the competition. I do – please vote!'

Afterwards, Niall took Minogue's criticism on the chin. '[She] gave us a bad comment but we're going to get bad comments,' he said. 'So we've got to take it on board and improve it next week.' Niall showed that the cocky lad who auditioned in Dublin was already maturing into a more considered and poised personality.

Week Eight
Theme: Rock

This was the week that Harry's ascendancy within the band's pecking order neared its peak. Although Liam still took plenty of the vocals for their opening track of the two-song night, the very choice of song was Harry's. They sang 'Summer of '69', a song Harry had sung as a boy. With the song choice presented on-air as entirely Harry's doing, he was getting plenty of attention. Already, it had been reported that Harry had come up with the name of the band, after commenting that they were all 'headed in one direction'. He also led the band on their mid-song walkabout and as they returned to the stage it was he who was positioned in the middle for the song's conclusion. It was as if a musical changing of the guard was occurring. Walsh told them: 'Hey, boys – it absolutely worked! I love the choice of song, I love the vibe, the vitality you bring to the competition. The competition would not be the same without One Direction.' Amen to that, thought a nation of young female viewers. Minogue was more positive than the previous week, saying: 'You've clearly done lots of work and really stepped it up, I like that.' Cole was stunned by the audience hysteria, saying: 'We've got feet stamps going on, there's electricity in the room, it's fantastic.'

However, it was Cowell whose comments were most significant. 'I had nothing to do with this song choice – Harry chose the song, great choice of song,' he said. As Harry beamed his winning smile he was congratulated by his band mates, with Niall even toying with Harry's famous curly locks. With the semi-final looming the following week, Cowell reminded the boys – but essentially the audience – that they had 'worked your butts off to get where you've got to', and implored the audience once more to, 'Please – pick up the phone!'

It should have been good times for the band. Everyone looked happy again – except for one member. Liam, perhaps feeling relegated by the attention and increasing prominence of Harry, was notably long-faced and seemed downcast as O'Leary continued the Harry love-fest. As O'Leary read out the number for viewers to call to vote for One Direction, Liam was the only member not smiling. He toyed with his microphone at one point but was otherwise a picture of despondency.

For the second song, they crooned 'You Are So Beautiful'. It was difficult to argue with the producers' decision to increasingly focus on Harry, as he tenderly sang his lines, the camera zooming close on his boyish face, his eyes the definition of boy band dolefulness. Walsh told them that the song had proven that they are 'a great vocal group – everyone in this group can sing'. Minogue told them they were 'stunning' and Cole added that she felt they had 'a really bright future'. Cowell told them, 'in many ways that was my favourite performance from you', and singled Zayn out for praise.

The public voted for them again in sufficient numbers to put them straight through. They were in the semi-finals!

The Semi-final

Their first track was a twist on Rihanna's monster hit 'Only Girl (in the World)'. By this

161

stage in the competition the band had become so polished that they no longer took to the stage as the plucky, freshly formed underdogs, unable to believe their luck. Instead they carried themselves as a band proper – with all the solidity and confidence that entails. As they promised to make the subject of the song the only girl in the world, schoolgirls across the nation wished that they were that girl. Walsh told them: 'Week after week, you're getting better and better, and you bring hysteria to the show. If there is any justice you will absolutely be in the final – you deserve to be in the final.' Minogue was again less sycophantic in her comment. 'Guys, I hope you never let us down because I really wanna see you guys as the next big boy band,' she began. Taking her role as a judge seriously, she then offered some constructive criticism, telling them: 'I have to say, some weeks you come out and I think it's very samey. That one was brilliant – you really stepped it up for the semi-finals.'

Cole then spoke of her part in the band's week, during which she had effectively stood in for Cowell who had been absent. 'This week, for me, I got to know you all a little bit better because your mentor wasn't here,' she said. 'I thoroughly enjoyed mentoring you ... but that song for me was a little bit dangerous because it's so current right now as Rihanna's record that you have to completely make it like it was never, ever written for her, and I don't know if it quite worked for me but I don't think it makes a difference. I hope to see you in the final.'

'Someone's being tactical!' said Cowell, referring to Cole's words. He then put in perspective the band's plight. Noting the huge increase in their stature, he felt moved to remind the viewers that the band would still need public votes. 'I've got to tell you guys, I know this is going to sound a bit biased but I thought this song was absolutely perfect for you because it is exactly what I liked about them: they didn't take the safe option. They chose something completely different: they had the guts to do it ... Can I just say, you hear all the applause and people at home might think you're safe but nobody is safe in this competition and I would urge anyone, please, if they want to see these boys in the final, please pick up the phone and vote for them because they deserve it.'

Their next song on the night was 'Chasing Cars', by Snow Patrol. It's yearning, emotional melody was the perfect vehicle to attract votes. Who, one wondered, could resist a cheeky vote for this band as they sang the moving hit? In the feedback, Walsh, as keen as ever to claim a part in the band's family, said: 'Liam, Zayn, Niall, Harry and Louis – I know your names! If there's any justice all the young kids will pick up their phones and they're going to vote One Direction – you deserve it!' Minogue added: 'Guys, you've got through a really tough week and that was such a classy, classy performance! You've just grown up in front of our eyes ...' Cole said: 'This week I was so impressed, you didn't have Zayn, Simon wasn't around, you showed a real level of maturity and you really deserve a place in the final.'

Cowell said: 'Guys, Tim, who's been working with you all week, told me that you made a decision this morning to get in at eight in the morning so you could give yourselves more rehearsal time, and that's what it's all about. It's not about excuses, it's about having that great work ethic, picking yourselves up after what was a very tough week, and I said this before – I genuinely mean this – I am proud of you as people as much as I am artists. That was a great performance – good for you.' Good for them indeed: to their immense delight, the public vote sent them through to the following weekend's final. Along with Matt Cardle, Cher Lloyd and Rebecca Ferguson they would battle it out to be crowned *X Factor* champion. Was a band about to win the show for the first time?

However, behind the smiles, glitz and excitement, there was a family tragedy haunting Zayn. His grandfather, described by Zayn as a happy, jovial and entertaining character, had died during the week. Zayn had travelled home to Bradford to be with his loved ones as they came to terms with the shock and grief of their loss. The fact that Zayn had returned to London to sing on the live show had impressed a lot of those involved with the series – not least Cowell. Zayn's fellow band members rallied round him as he mourned – they even accompanied him when he travelled home for the funeral. Zayn truly appreciated this supportive and loving gesture.

Popularity, unity and form: as far as the contest itself went, everything was coming together at just the right time for One Direction.

The Final

The band's prospects were, on the face of it, strong going into the final. The hysteria of their fan base was deafening and the band had followed the golden rule of *X Factor* success: to peak later rather than earlier. Among those who were tipping them to win were former *X Factor* champions Joe McElderry – the Geordie singer whose success had spurred several members of One Direction to enter the show – and Alexandra Burke. However, a poll published in the *Sun* newspaper on the morning of the final had them as a distant third behind Rebecca Ferguson and the poll's predicted winner, Matt Cardle.

In the week before the big showdown the remaining finalists made the customary journeys to their respective hometowns. These always made for compelling and emotional television –

they also serve to galvanize the 'home' support for each act. Though, due to snow, the band did not travel to Niall's Ireland, they visited the hometowns of the other members, including Liam's Wolverhampton where they performed in front of five thousand people. Liam said the experience was 'absolutely awesome – the crowd were absolutely amazing'. He was also amazed that the frenzy was so intense that police were needed to hold the fans back. The band was 'buzzing', he remembered later. Harry added that it was, 'really exciting for us to think we're going to be doing loads of little gigs like that and some to bigger crowds than that'.

On the big night the band tried to put the newspaper poll out of their minds and focus on the task in hand. The final would take place over two nights, with performances and public voting spread over both nights. The first song they sang was 'Your Song', by Elton John. With their rival contestants singing less popularly known tracks, the band hoped that this classic, widely known choice would shore up their vote. For this song, Liam got his personal moment in the limelight – quite literally, as for the first verse of the song he stood alone on the dark stage, lit by a single light. It was the culmination of a personal journey for him: from his 2008 *X Factor* experience, which ended in rejection at the judges' houses phase, to now, standing almost as a solo artist on the stage of the *X Factor* final.

By the end of the first chorus the band had united behind a row of microphones, with Harry taking the central one. With snowfall, bright white lighting and a choir of white-clothed singers joining them for the finale of the song, the producers had thrown nearly every *X Factor* cliché at the performance. Walsh was as impressed as ever: 'Hey, One Direction, you're in the final – I hope you're here tomorrow night,' he said. 'It's amazing how five guys have gelled so well. I know you're all best friends. I've never seen a band cause so much hysteria so early in their career. I definitely think that you've got an amazing future. Niall, everybody in Ireland must vote for Niall, yes!'

Minogue echoed Walsh's wish. 'Guys, you have worked so hard in this competition. You were thrown together, you deserve to be here and I'd love to see you in the final tomorrow,' she said. Cowell said that the first two performances by Cardle and Ferguson were 'so good' that his 'heart was sinking' over his band's potential on the night. However, he said, the band 'gave it 1,000 per cent', and added, 'it's been an absolute pleasure working with you'. Lest his contribution sound like an obituary, bookmarking the band's *X Factor* experience, he added: 'I really hope people bother to pick up the phone, put you through to tomorrow because you deserve to be there'.

The intensity of the evening was almost unbearable. One thing no critic could take away from the series is that it knows how to perfectly build the tension of the final weekend. The excitement soared anew when the finalists performed their duets. Cardle sang with Rihanna, Lloyd with Will.i.am of the Black Eyed Peas and Ferguson with Christina Aguilera – all highly prestigious artists. However, One Direction felt that they had the pick of the lot: Robbie Williams. The man who had influenced them so much was about to join them to sing on primetime television.

Lest anyone not immediately grasp how thrilling this was for the band, their faces radiated with excitement, pride and almost disbelief as he joined them during their rendition of 'She's the One'. Each of the boys looked so happy it was impossible for viewers' hearts not to melt. Even Zayn smiled. The fact the duet went so smoothly was a relief to all. When Williams had sung with a previous finalist, Olly Murs, he had fluffed his cue, besmirching what should have been one of that final's key moments of drama. Williams had also endured a mishap-ridden performance on the show earlier in that series, when the doors failed to open on time for his dramatic stage entrance to sing his comeback single 'Bodies', making his eventual appearance somewhat frenzied.

As his successful duet with One Direction ended, he shouted, 'The lads – One Direction! Phone-in!' and then all six disappeared briefly into a group hug. Robbie even lifted Niall into the air. Louis said he was: 'An absolutely massive Robbie fan – thank you so much for doing this with us.' To which Robbie casually replied, 'Oh it's a pleasure – you guys rock!' Harry, looking more serious than ever, spoke of the 'pleasure it had been to sing with Robbie'. Cowell described Robbie as 'a great friend to the show – very, very generous with his time and he's made these boys' night of their lives.' The excitement was enough to send the band through the first public vote of the weekend. It was Cher Lloyd who was sent home, leaving One Direction to battle it out with Cardle and Ferguson the following evening.

On Sunday, the stakes were as high as ever. In what would be their final performance of the series, One Direction sang 'Torn'. As the song they had sung at judges' houses, this was an emotional choice. It reminded the lads themselves – as well as the audience – of how far they had come. Their opponents, Cardle and Ferguson, sang Katy Perry's 'Firework' and Eurythmics' 'Sweet Dreams' respectively. The next count of the votes would eliminate one of the three, leaving the final two to battle it out.

The final judges' verdicts for the band were all upbeat, but were for the most part phrased in expectation that this was the end of the road in the competition. 'You've got brilliant chemistry, I love the harmonies. I love the song choice and we've got five new pop stars!' Walsh told them. Minogue added: 'Guys, you've done all the right things to make your place here in the final. That was a fantastic performance. Whatever happens tonight, I'm sure you guys are going to go on and release records and be the next big band.' Cole, in particular, sounded a conclusive note, saying: 'It's been so lovely to watch you guys from your first audition. To think that was only a few months ago! I really believe that you've got a massive future ahead of you and I wanna say "thank you" for being such lovely guys to be around.' Only Simon Cowell, predictably, spoke of the band surviving the next cull and winning the show. 'Let's be clear: anyone who comes into this final has got a great chance of bettering their future,' he said. 'But this is a competition and in terms of the competition, in terms of who's worked the hardest, who I think deserves to win based on the future of something we haven't seen before. I would love to hear your names read out at the end of the competition – because I think you deserve it.'

With Cher Lloyd already gone, the weekend had thus far conformed to the prediction in the

Sun poll. If that conformity continued, then One Direction would leave the show at this stage. With Matt Cardle and Dannii Minogue on the left of the stage and Rebecca Ferguson and Cheryl Cole on the right, the One Direction boys were in the middle, standing with Simon Cowell. Complete with the customary, agonizing dramatic pauses, Dermot O'Leary announced that first Cardle and then Ferguson were through, which left One Direction out of the remainder of the contest.

Cowell was the first to react to the disappointing news. He looked distraught, almost angry, as he turned his back on proceedings. It was the body language of disgust. The boys looked absolutely devastated. As one Tweeter commented: 'It is like looking through a kaleidoscope at a distraught Justin Bieber.'

Louis, befittingly as the band's oldest member, was the first to speak following this crushing blow. 'It's been absolutely incredible,' he said. 'For me, the highlight was when we first sang together at the judges' houses. That was unbelievable. And you know what? We've done our absolute best, we've worked hard.'

Zayn, looking to the future, added a defiant note. 'We're definitely going to stay together, this isn't the last of One Direction!' he said, to the absolute joy of their fans across the country, whose hearts had sunk when the boys' exit was confirmed.

The show, though, had to go on without One Direction, who watched from the wings. When Cardle was named the winner, the boys were delighted for him. As he sang his winners' song, 'When We Collide', the other finalists ran to join him on the stage. The celebratory mob that ensues at this point is always a moving part of the final – it has been a tradition since the final of the first series of *Pop Idol* in 2002. The members of One Direction were as lively as anyone during the massed huddle around Cardle. The ever-bubbly Niall was first out of the throng to embrace the winner, who looked stunned but delighted.

As Cardle was swallowed up by the throng, Harry sang the lyrics back to him while Niall moved to the front of the stage to whip-up the audience into ever more frenzied cheering and singing. It really was bedlam, and the best – or worst, in the eyes of some – moment was yet to come. As O'Leary wrapped up the evening and the series itself, the camera caught Harry whispering something to the triumphant Cardle. Not everybody could make out what Harry had said but some eagle-eyed viewers thought that they had.

Within moments, Twitter was flooded with messages speculating that what Harry had said was: 'Just think how much pussy you're going to get.' This theory was picked up by the mainstream media and provoked a combination of outrage, amusement and approval from differing sectors of the British public. Though Harry initially kept his counsel over what he had said, he would, in time, confirm that he had indeed made the bawdy remark, but not before the subject had been dubbed 'pussygate'. In the meantime, his mother was so angry that she grounded him when he got home.

Looking back over the series in an interview with *Digital Spy*, Harry returned to more family-friendly vocabulary. 'When we walked in and saw the studio for the first time. Then when us five stood behind the doors for the first time on the live show, for that first song – for me that was the best moment. That was where we were actually doing it, the real thing, for the first time. That was a big moment.' Would they even have believed, at that moment in week one, that they would make it all the way to the final? Though their disappointment at not winning the show was huge, it was matched by pride in the fact that they had done so well.

Their pride was well deserved. There was just one small, but ever so important, question in their minds: what next?

8 WHAT MAKES THEM BEAUTIFUL

After they had been eliminated, the band was called to a private meeting with Cowell. 'I've made a decision,' he told them, then embarked on a dramatic pause – it must have felt as if they were back on-air! Finally, he told them what that decision was: he was going to sign them up to his division of Sony Records. Good old 'Uncle Simon' had shown that, even when the cameras are not trained on him, he cannot resist leaving people hanging on his decisions. When his decisions are frequently of such a monumental nature, it must be hard to resist hamming it up a bit, even if that leaves hopefuls almost breathless with anticipation.

Anyway, for the band this was the news they had longed to hear. Though many commentators had speculated that Cowell would indeed sign the band whether they won the contest or not, none of the boys had taken that for granted. They knew that the entertainment industry is a ruthless and fickle one in which tough decisions are made regardless of the feelings of the players. As they heard the news their emotions were so strong that Harry burst into tears – his cool persona entirely forgotten in the midst of the moment. Then they could not wait to tell their parents. Like many performers, the boys are keen to make their parents proud.

Cowell told the band: 'You have to enjoy yourselves. You're going to make a lot of money, but you have to enjoy every single minute of it.' Though the guys did not realize this straightaway, Cowell had almost made a noteworthy sacrifice. He felt that he had such a promising prospect on his hands that he invited other divisions of Sony to make their own presentations to him before he decided where to send the boys. Rather than automatically signing them to his division, he was willing to consider handing them elsewhere. He explained why to *Rolling Stone*. 'This was such an important signing, we let three or four of the Sony labels make a presentation,' he said. 'I didn't automatically give it to my own label. I thought, "This is so important, if somebody can come up with a better idea …" I was actually willing to pass them along to another division of Sony because I thought the group were that important.'

Triumphant, the band then went their separate ways for Christmas. Though they were given less than a week off for the festive season, they were just glad to be at home with their loved ones – a haven of familiar serenity during a frantic and unfamiliar time. As they celebrated with their families, the boys could take a considered look at how much their lives had changed over the past year.

They were also getting a crash course in the realities of fame. While out shopping over the Christmas break, Zayn had brought a shopping centre to a virtual standstill within a minute or two of him being first recognized. Harry, meanwhile, noted an almost perpetual gathering of fans near his family home. This was his first encounter with such intrusive fandom: and he found himself worrying about them catching a cold.

Around the same time, Louis heard that some fellow Doncastrians were to be heard scowling that he was unworthy of the fame and success he had achieved. This is typical of the provincial sniping that people who better themselves sometimes face. It should be seen for what it is: envy and confirmation that you are on the up. At the time, though, it can be hard to take, particularly for one as young as Louis. Just weeks earlier Louis had faced similar comments from former *X Factor* winner Steve Brookstein. The middle-aged crooner, who has taken his own fall from fame notoriously badly, wrote on Twitter that Louis was the 'luckiest man in music' for landing a record deal. He was about to become one of the first people to encounter the full wrath of the One Direction fans.

As the fans raged at Brookstein on Twitter, Louis' mother Johanna sent him a pointed message herself. 'Hi, I'm Louis's mum,' she wrote. 'My family have always liked you and bought your records. Why be so cruel? Why shame him in public? He was sad about his audition. He was incredibly nervous. Listen to his YouTube. He is eighteen Steve! I honestly thought you were a nice bloke. Sadly for us now what we were told about you seems accurate.' Brookstein was unrepentant, replying: 'If you are Louis's mum. Get the poor lad some singing lessons for Christmas. A couple of dozen at least.' As Twitter neared meltdown due to the sheer weight of Tweets being fired by the fans, Brookstein remained unfazed. 'Listen, he is a rogue trader,' he wrote. 'A Mickey Mouse cowboy builder. Don't blame me for exposing his poor workmanship. End of.' Louis responded with dignity, telling Brookstein: 'Steve you're my idol!' It was a classy response to taunting delivered by a man old enough to be his father.

With their welcome, yet all too brief, Christmas break over, One Direction reunited in London. Their first significant professional task for 2011 was not the hardest one. As mere mortals crunched through cold mornings to school, college or work, One Direction escaped the harsh British winter by flying to the warmer climes of the West Coast of America. They spent five days in Los Angeles – the self-declared capital of the entertainment industry. There, the sun was shining and the city was glittering with stars. The time was spent in a combination of work – including a recording session in a studio and a meeting with leading producer Max Martin – sightseeing and shopping.

On their return to Britain at the end of January, the band had their most extreme encounter with their fans to date, as they were confronted with hundreds of screaming fans when they arrived at Heathrow Airport. Security staff had to grab the band and escort them at great speed to a police van, just to avoid them being mobbed by the fans. It was a crazy experience and the band members responded in different ways. Louis, for example, 'got a real buzz' from it, but Niall was completely freaked out.

A humorous aside occurred in the shape of former Boyzone lead singer, Ronan Keating, a heartthrob himself back in the 1990s, who was arriving around the same time. Once upon a time he had faced scenes such as this. He wrote on Twitter: 'Just landed at Heathrow and when

I walked out there were hundreds of screaming fans sadly not for me HaHa. One Direction were on flight.' Still, the experience will have brought back fond memories for Keating.

Next on the agenda for the band was their part in *The X Factor* tour, where even more screaming girls would be present to threaten their eardrums. Joining most of the other finalists from the series, they performed in arenas across the country to the show's most dedicated fans. They were put through their paces in the days before the tour – they had to learn new dance moves and also prepare some patter for between the songs. The rehearsals and the drilling were serious: they went over some parts of their slot over twenty times. These were tough days at the Light Structures venue in Wakefield, but the effort was well worth it.

On the tour they shared a dressing room with the other male artists. This meant that they were reunited with Matt Cardle, Aidan Grimshaw and even the comical Wagner. It made for a crowded and energy-filled room as they laughed, remembering the funny times during the series, and also looked to their respective futures. After each show they would head to their hotel, often pouring themselves into the bar to party the rest of the night away. On two separate occasions they ended up having 'fruit fights'. The first, in Sheffield, lasted for five anarchic minutes. It kicked off when Louis casually tried to launch an apple core into the bin. There was a 'second leg' fruit fight in Liverpool. No wonder Harry said that he never wanted the tour to end. Vegetables also played a comical part in the tour. After Louis had jokingly commented in an interview that the sort of girls he goes for are girls who like eating carrots, they were bombarded with carrots by the fans. Girls would arrive at their shows and appearances waving banners featuring carrots, wearing carrot T-shirts and carrying handfuls of the vegetables themselves. During one of the concerts Louis even took to the stage wearing a carrot costume. As Louis later joked, all these carrots around him meant he was now able to 'see in the dark'!

Onstage, they loved every moment. From the opening night in Birmingham, when the deafening noise from the 12,000-strong crowd that greeted them blew the boys away, through the other cities, including in Ireland, it was an experience they would never forget. It also served as a useful apprenticeship for the touring experience. In the future, they would fill venues just as large – and even larger – than those on the *X Factor* tour. Generally, successful bands slowly build their live career from small venues to medium sized and then the biggies, rather than selling out massive arenas on their first tour. So it was of enormous help that the boys had already had these tasters of being on stage in front of such huge crowds.

Their key memories of the tour will include the several occasions that Liam's trousers ripped onstage. It was always during their rendition of 'Forever Young' that his 'wardrobe malfunctions' occurred. Safe to say, none of the girls in the audience were about to ask for their money back! At the wrap party, which was held in a hotel nightclub after the final performance, the crew, management and artists fondly bid farewell to the tour and each other. The tour had established that the biggest party animals of the band were Harry and Louis, with most onlookers agreeing that Louis probably pipped Harry for the championship. One thing they all loved equally on the tour was food: the Nando's chicken restaurant chain does very well out of One Direction.

In a foreshadowing of the hectic schedule that awaited them, the band were involved with other projects during the tour. The most significant one was the filming of a television advertisement for the Nintendo DS Pokemon product. The advert was hardly strenuous work for the band. It was shot in a hotel room and essentially simply featured them playing around. The homely Louis was utterly chuffed by the fact that part of the deal was they were each given a free DS Pokemon. Another promotional project they were involved with at this time was the release of their first official book, *Forever Young*. Frenzied signing appearances helped push sales of the title ever higher – it ended up quite a hit in the bestseller charts. With other books published about the band in the months after the series, One Direction were in a strange position: they were a pop band with more books than records to their names. This was about to change.

With the tour over, the band took a bit of time off. Niall headed to Spain with his father and a friend; Liam went to Florida with his parents; Louis and Harry went skiing in Courchevel in the French Alps.

On their return, they were ushered into the studio to record their debut single. The song that had been carefully chosen for them was 'What Makes You Beautiful'. It begins with a brief, staccato guitar riff, with an up-tempo, almost cheeky feel to it, reminiscent of the early material of McFly. Then the sound of a drumstick on a cymbal ushers in the first verse. Liam's voice is heard first. In deep, semi-raunchy tones and through an accent tinged with American, he delivers the attention-grabbing opening line. The backing track becomes richer for the bridge, sung by Harry. His soulful, dreamy voice is at its best as he leads the track to its explosive chorus. At which point the full, anthemic quality of the track becomes clear.

In verse two the song takes a slight detour in style. Zayn's delivery takes in a degree of rap and gives the song a touch – though only a light touch – of 'edge'. Harry's bridge then takes us back to the chorus. Following which, that classic pop trick of a 'na na-na na' chant is deployed until the *a cappella* middle-eight, which Harry sings. It is an unexpected moment of quiet and calm – all the better to precede the final chorus, which crashes in supremely. Both in the video and in live performances the band whip up the audience during the chorus. It is not a song that should end with a fade – and neither does it. Instead, a final 'That's what makes you beautiful' from Harry closes the three minutes and eighteen seconds of pop perfection.

It was a shrewdly selected opening track for the band, setting them apart from British boy bands of recent times, and avoiding both the ballad-heavy, key-change centric image of Westlife and the faux, laddish feel of The Wanted. Instead, it played to the strength of the members of One Direction: it was at once mischievous, young, flippant, profound and uplifting. Never had a generation of girls been more inclined to flip their hair.

Written by Rami Yacoub, Carl Falk and Savan Kotecha, who between them have written for Westlife, Britney Spears, Nicki Minaj, Usher and Celine Dion, it was, in truth, pretty much teen pop gold. Musically, its chord progression is bright and its production, masterminded by Yacoub and Falk, soundly simplistic. Praise must go to those behind the track as well as those who selected it for One Direction: songs such as this, which so perfectly both capture and define the spirit of teenage pop, might sound easy to produce but they are not.

The boys understood all this only too well. 'When we were recording in the studio we knew instantly that we wanted this track to be our first single,' Harry told Digital Spy, adding, 'I think for us we wanted to release something that wasn't cheesy but it was fun. It kind of represented us, I think it took us a while to find it but I think we found the right song.' Liam, too, felt it was right up their street. 'We always wanted [the debut single] to be something that people didn't expect and then when we heard it, it wasn't what we expected either, so it kind of fitted perfectly.' The release was surrounded by pressure, too, something the boys were more than aware of. 'There's a lot of expectation,' said Louis. 'All the fans know we've been busy recording, so there's a bit of pressure.'

The sound was attributed to a wide range of influences. As well as the aforementioned McFly, they also claimed nods at the style of acts as diverse as American pop giants 'N Sync, 1970s prog-rock dinosaurs Pink Floyd and the Mexican pop-folk classic 'La Bamba'. Example and Calvin Harris were two other acts mentioned in this sense. Many also noted a connection between the opening riff and that of the *Grease* track, 'Summer Loving'. There was a pleasant serendipity here, as some of the boys had appeared in school productions of that very musical.

On its release, on 11 September 2011, the critics were thrilled. Summing up the theme of the song as one that showed that the band's 'favourite sort' of lady is: 'That endangered breed who are visually stunning but aren't aware of it', online entertainment website Digital Spy's Robert Copsey heaped praise on the track. Giving it four out of five stars, he declared it a cross between Pink and McFly, concluding: 'Like a Forever Friends bear from your high school crush, it's adorable, completely innocent and bound to cause a stir amongst your mates.'

As a website that lives for reality television and its graduates, Digital Spy could be expected to look on the song favourably. A less expected champion of it was the *NME*, in which Ailbhe Malone declared it as 'so unthreatening it might have to think twice about holding hands, lest it get overwhelmed'. However, she said this was not 'a bad thing'.

Taking an unsurprisingly technical musical look at the song, Malone continued: 'Channelling their sterling performance of "My Life Would Suck Without You", "What Makes You Beautiful" is exuberant with a catchy "oh na na na" middle eight. The real genius is that the chord progression is simple enough to be played on an acoustic guitar at a house party.' The children's TV *Newsround* website gave the single four stars out of five, saying: 'Think summer, think sunshine, think parties on the beach with your mates, and you'll get the general vibe of "What Makes You Beautiful". It's classic pop – fun, upbeat and incredibly catchy.' As we shall see, it was not just the critics, nor even just the record-buying public, that loved the song – so too did award bodies.

First, though, let us take a look at its commercial performance, something the band could hardly wait to see. 'I'm excited because it's what I've been working towards all my life and it's finally happening,' Zayn told *Top of the Pops* magazine, ahead of the single's release. By the time it was released such a juggernaut of expectation had been created for it that there was no doubt it would be a big hit. Three weeks ahead of the release date, Sony Music announced that the single had already broken all records for the numbers of pre-orders for a label act in the company's history – quite an achievement when you consider that Sony is the home of international superstars including Michael Jackson, Beyoncé and Christina Aguilera. On release, the song debuted at number one in Britain and Ireland. In due course it would perform very well in other territories, too.

The promotional video for the song is, of course, a considerable part of its success. This part of any band's image has been important since the dawn of MTV in the 1980s. However, in the modern internet age the video's importance has assumed a new dimension: thanks to YouTube and social networking sites, management can, to an extent, bypass the mainstream media and market their videos direct to the fans. One Direction had filmed their single's video over two days in July, in Malibu, California. Directed by director, cinematographer and photographer John Urbano, in it they are seen frolicking on the beach, driving a campervan, playing with a football and much more besides. Their fun is infectious. As he delivers the line about flipping hair in the first chorus, Harry flips his own much-loved curly mane.

A group of young ladies join the fun a minute or so in, but it's when the band take their tops off to play in the ocean that the interest of most viewers will increase. The fact that there are but a few brief scenes of their topless torsos was deliberate. This was less a tease and more a determination on the part of the band's management to not overly sexualize them at this early stage of their career. Noting, for example, the way that Justin Bieber had first conquered the world of pop with a basically squeaky-clean and wholesome image, the management were determined that One Direction should not leap out of their clothes at the first moment as other boy bands had done.

The most intimate moment of the video comes when Harry sings the *a cappella* part up close and personally to one of the female models. It is, in truth, a slightly awkward moment. Harry looks fairly – but not entirely – comfortable. The actress, though, seems far less at home and, the fans will have noted with passion, not entirely thrilled to be in such a scene. The shoots for pop videos can be lengthy and tiring experiences, so hopefully the fans – who would have killed to have been in her shoes that day – can forgive her.

Meanwhile, the band had more promotional appearances to fulfil. Their first major television interview appearance was on Channel 4's *Alan Carr: Chatty Man*. With the help of Carr's considerable wit and outrageous chatter, the band's personalities came across well. They managed to dispel the suspicion held by some members of the public that boy band members are vapid and dull characters. Instead, they had the audience in stitches. Harry in particular was oozing charisma on the night. Naturally,

Carr was not going to allow Harry to get away without quizzing him about 'pussygate'. Harry's tongue-in-cheek explanation will linger long in the memory. 'I was completely innocent!' he said. 'Me and Matt had been discussing Christmas presents for our parents and Matt had previously said he wanted to get as many cats as he could for his mum. So when he won I told him to think about how many cats he could get now.' Nobody was buying that explanation for one moment, but everyone was laughing at Harry's inventiveness.

Other highlights of the band's romping slot on the show included Niall's amazingly convincing imitation of *X Factor* announcer Peter Dickson's voice, and Louis' funny tales of American car mishaps. Carr also asked Louis about Brookstein's online attack on him. 'Does your mum always come and defend you?' asked the host. Louis, to everyone's amusement, had to admit that she did. Carr had the boys in stitches when he inquired about a possible dalliance between Harry and a model from their video called Madison. 'Did you take a trip down Madison's avenue?' he asked, much to the band's boyish delight.

The band also performed their single on the Cowell-created game show *Red or Black*. This appearance turned out to be a less happy experience. For part of the song the audience were shown a specially acted VT of the band travelling to the television studio by underground, singing the first two versus and choruses on the tube among the fans, and then being chased from the underground station, down the road to the TV studio by screaming fans. What was meant as a simple fun gimmick was instead interpreted by some viewers as evidence that the band were being shielded from giving a full performance due to a supposed lack of talent when it came to live performance.

One would have thought that seeing Harry clearly sing the *a cappella* section live onstage, should have been enough to dispel those thoughts. His nerves – and breathlessness having danced around on-stage – were both clear. His hands shook as he sang and his eyes looked more than a little anxious. Had he got the timing wrong the whole performance would have become an embarrassing flop. When he completed the solo part successfully he breathed a sigh of relief, Niall patted him on the shoulder and the band launched back into the full crashing chorus. It had all been all right on the night – or had it?

When they came off air, Harry said he 'felt a little sorry for himself' over the way he had let his nerves show. He logged onto Twitter and searched to see what was being said about him online. He was devastated by the extent of the abuse that he found. Louis tried to comfort him but realized there was not much he could do. 'I felt powerless', said Louis later.

The band rallied round Harry and assured him that they and the fans still adored him. Indeed, for many fans Harry's nerves had only made him seem more real and adorable. It reminded the fans that this was a new band comprising of young men. One Direction were on the way to becoming the top dogs of British pop but they retained the image of the underdog. They were being styled and managed well. Since they left *The X Factor* they had been physically transformed only to an extent: they looked and behaved more like pop stars but were still recognizable as the boys who had appeared for their first auditions. Next up for One Direction was the moment that was what it was all about.

Called *Up All Night*, One Direction's debut album was a carefully selected, brilliantly produced piece of work. It begins with the aforementioned 'What Makes You Beautiful'. In an album with several surprises and changes of pace, the first occurs with track two: in contrast to the opener, 'It's Gotta Be You' is a classic boy band ballad. Here, the lyrics are full of regret for hurt that has been unintentionally caused. Who cannot relate to the expressed wish that time could be rewound? Gorgeous strings turn this into an epic affair that delights the listener – it is no wonder it was chosen as a subsequent single.

Track three is essentially a return to the impish, pop-rock atmosphere of the opener. 'One Thing' is the natural sibling to 'What Makes You Beautiful'. In many ways, the lyrics mirror their own story – when they sing that they need that one thing, the one thing the girl in the song has, they could be singing of themselves, for they have that indefinable one thing that Simon Cowell and the music industry itself needed. 'More Than This', the slowest and most gentle track on the album, features some astonishing falsetto vocals, which show the range of the band and add true gravitas to the experience. The song is also notable for a fine solo from Louis, whose performance is a fair response to the online sniping that went on in the previous year.

Track five is the album's title tune, 'Up All Night', and is a vivid call to arms to the party generation. 'I Wish' is a mid-tempo sound very much in the 'album track' mode: there is nothing wrong with it, but it does not leap out at the listener; while 'Tell Me a Lie' is a song that reeks of America: if ever a song on the album was made to be listened to with the roof down on a US freeway, this is it. Its successor, 'Taken', is, in contrast, one to be sung around a bonfire, complete with acoustic guitars. Harry has arguably never sounded better than he does on this track in which the boys are defiant rather than doting: 'Who do you think you are?' they ask, a hint of menace in their voices.

If the next song, 'I Want', reminds the listener of a mid-career track by McFly, that is for good reason as it was written by their chief songwriter, Tom Fletcher. Despite making some unflattering remarks about One Direction when they first came to the public eye, Fletcher quickly noted their commercial potential and happily handed them this song. 'Everything About You' is far more electro and mainstream pop in sound. Some strong lyrics lift it out of the pack, again underscoring the attention that has gone into the entire album.

'Same Mistakes' is a sweet, rolling ballad, the rich backing track smoothly enhancing the vocals. With the penultimate track, the band say they want to save a girl from her current lot in life. As such, 'Save You Tonight', a song that could easily be performed by JLS or The Wanted, pushes multiple buttons. Few fans would resist such salvation from these lads. For a moment, when the final track kicks in, the listener's ear is tricked into wondering if it is a cover of Taio Cruz's 'Dynamite'. Then, during the bridge, the song momentarily reminds one of Rihanna's 'Only Girl (in the World)'. An impressive anthem ending an impressive album.

To bring the album to fruition, the band had worked with a string of big names, Wayne Hector, the man who wrote Westlife's mega hit 'Flying Without Wings', being one of them. Another was Steve Robson, who had worked with James Morrison and Busted. Perhaps the two people they worked with who most excited the boys were RedOne, who has co-produced a string of hits for Lady Gaga, and Ed Sheeran, the ginger-haired singer-songwriter sensation.

'Getting to write and record with Ed Sheeran on our album was an honour,' said Niall. Harry agreed, commenting that the people they worked with on the album were 'legendary'. Liam, meanwhile, was delighted to work with 'hit machine' Claude Kelly, the man behind 'Grenade'. They recorded it in both the UK and America, and in all there were twenty-two songwriters involved in the tracks. On top of this, the band members themselves get co-writing credits on three of the album's tracks.

The album debuted at number two in the UK charts. Impressive in itself – and things became still more impressive when it became the fastest-selling debut album on the UK Albums Chart of 2011. It also reached the top 10 in other countries including Sweden, Ireland, Netherlands, New Zealand and Australia. (On its release in America in March 2012, the album went straight to number one, making One Direction the first British band in US chart history to achieve this with their debut album.) The *Sun*'s face of showbiz Gordon Smart declared: '*Up All Night* will be lapped up by their young fan-base' and praised it for its blend of sounds and styles. *Cosmopolitan* magazine felt that the album was full of 'toe-tappers that are just impossible to dislike'; the *Independent* newspaper said the album would 'sell by the zillion'; while the *Daily Star* said it was full of 'belting fun pop anthems'.

In the wake of the album's release, One Direction took to the road on their first headline tour. Beginning in the middle of December in Watford, they played in cities across the UK and Ireland in shows that had sold-out of tickets within minutes of them going on sale. As well as singing tracks from their album and the B-side 'Na, Na, Na', they also performed some covers. Among these were 'I Gotta Feeling', by Black Eyed Peas, The Zutons/Amy Winehouse track 'Valerie' and 'Use Somebody' by Kings of Leon. There were also 'snowball' fights with the plastic snowballs that were sent down from on high at one point in the set, followed later by silver streamers. With Niall plucking on his acoustic guitar for parts of the set and the band indulging in much between-track banter, the shows made for superb nights out. Naturally, the other ingredient of the experience was the screams of the fans lucky enough to get tickets. Even seasoned concert goers and staff at the venues were taken aback by the volume of the noise. The only downside of the tour came when a car smashed into their tour bus in early January. Although three of the band who were inside the bus at the time suffered head and neck pains, as well as shock, there were no serious injuries.

9 THE AMERICAN DREAM

Having been formed in 2010 and releasing a single and an album in 2011 One Direction wanted to up their game in 2012. The year of 2012 was believed by some to augur the end of the world, but One Direction wanted it to be the start of a whole new life for them. The prospect of becoming a one-minute wonder that would disappear as fast as they had appeared, haunted each member of the band. They wanted to be in the music industry for the long haul and to make their success a truly global concern. They were not even content to merely replicate the fun and success of 2011 – they wanted to soar ever higher and better it. Ahead of them were several significant opportunities to do just that. Starting with a trip to Britain's most prestigious music awards night: The BRITs.

Held at the O2 Arena in February, the BRIT Awards 2012 was hosted by Louis' old pal James Corden. It turned out to be an evening of highs and lows for the band. One of the lows would haunt them for months. First, though, came the high. They were nominated in the Best British Single category. Given how many successful bands never win a BRIT during their career, the fact that One Direction was already on the brink of winning their first was flushed with significance. For their category, a public vote had been held to decide the winner. It was listeners to Capital FM radio station who had voted, but in the excitement of winning the award, Harry thanked the listeners of Radio One by accident.

Their excitement as they were named winners was palpable. Onstage to present the award to them was pop star Tinie Tempah. 'Wow,' said Louis. 'We cannot believe that we are stood here.' He then added that, 'this award is for the fans'. Harry was next to speak. After echoing Louis' thanks to the fans, he added: 'And a massive thank you to Radio One'. Mindful of the enormous damage this could cause One Direction's chances of air-time on Capital, the band's PR firm issued a swift statement via Twitter. 'One Direction forgot to thank the Capital Radio listeners last night when picking up their BRIT Award for "Best British Single",' read the statement. 'This was an oversight as the boys were caught up in the excitement of winning. The band would like take this opportunity to thank Capital Radio and all their listeners for their support and for voting for them.'

Although Harry was kicking himself over his slip-up, he and his band mates tried hard to not let it get in the way of some serious celebration. Later that night they certainly appeared the worse for the wear. During an interview, Niall was flush-faced and Harry slurred and mumbled. When they reappeared for an even later interview, Harry said nothing but merely pointed at the camera in a rather vacant way. Asked how they would divide the single trophy between them, they joked they would either cut it into pieces or photocopy it. Later, Harry finally admitted that he did make the 'pussygate' comment. With his hard partying perhaps contributing to his mood of candour, he Tweeted: 'I admit … I did say "Think how much pussy you're gonna get" I apologize.' There were a few sore heads the next morning as they dissected what had been an eventful night.

During his part of their acceptance speech, Liam had mentioned that they were about to announce an arena tour. The band duly did just that, unveiling a string of dates, beginning at London's O2 Arena on 22 February 2013. The fifteen dates sold-out within a few minutes of going on sale. A list of twenty new shows was quickly added, including matinée performances in London, Cardiff, Manchester and Birmingham. The speed with which they could sell-out Britain's biggest arenas was incredible: One Direction were, by this measure, the kings of the UK pop scene.

If February 2012 had been fun, then March would be magnificent. They cracked the all important and almost impossible American market. When one looks at this list of top British and Irish acts that have failed to replicate their success stateside, one begins to appreciate the scale of the challenge. Among those who flopped there are Westlife, Robbie Williams, and

Oasis. Busted, then Britain's biggest pop band and an act huge in Japan, even made an MTV documentary, *America Or Busted* that focused on their inability to make it there. With bands who had ruled the British charts for years failing in America, who would have held out hope for One Direction there?

However, more or less immediately after they arrived in America for the big push, they found that they had a huge, fanatical and vocal following there. They were mobbed in Boston and, when they moved to Toronto in Canada, the police were called after a crowd so huge and excitable surrounded their hotel. The music industry journal *Billboard*, said: 'There's a lot of possibility here, there's a lot of upside ... that level of talent with those kinds of looks ... it's really a perfect storm for a massive, massive successful phenomenon.' Given how hard it can be to impress the US media, these were very promising words.

The band were finding that, rather than experiencing the fruitless and soul-destroying slog that many British bands encounter there, they were going down a treat. Comparisons were soon being made between the band and Britain's biggest ever musical export. Not only did One Direction get a slot on *Today*, the biggest breakfast television show in America, they were trailed on the show as a band akin to The Beatles. 'Now at 8.39 a.m., with the group that some people are saying are inspiring the next case of Beatlemania ...' said the presenter. 'Odds are, if you do have a teenager in your house, a pre-teen girl, she's already obsessed with One Direction.' The band duly appeared at the *Today Show* plaza, in the shadow of New York's iconic Rockefeller Center. They also appeared on that other landmark US television show, *Saturday Night Live*. Hugely successful and established bands that had never quite made it onto either show could only look on with envy.

'What Makes You Beautiful' first charted in America at number 28 – the highest *Billboard* Hot 100 debut for a UK act for fourteen years. This was exciting enough in itself, but even better news was just around the corner. Just stop for a moment and imagine the joy all round when they were told that they had become the first UK pop group to debut at number one on the US *Billboard* album chart with *Up All Night*. They were stunned and humbled by the news. 'We simply cannot believe that we are number one in America,' said Harry. 'It's beyond a dream come true for us. We want to thank each and every one of our fans in the US who bought our album and we would also like to thank the American public for being so supportive of us.' Niall added: 'As you can imagine, we are over the moon'. Their mentor and surrogate uncle, Simon Cowell, was bursting with pride. 'I couldn't be happier for One Direction, it is an incredible achievement,' he wrote on his Twitter account. 'They deserve it. They have the best fans in the world.'

This was not only exciting for One Direction and their fans, it was a moment of pride for Britain. They were not the only British boy band making a big splash in America. The Wanted were also proving a hit there: their single 'Glad You Came' peaked at number 4 on the *Billboard* Hot 100. Even better news came when American fans of One Direction explained that they loved the band not in spite of them being British but because of it. 'It just makes them cuter', said one.

Later, in his interview with *Rolling Stone* magazine, Simon Cowell put into context how they had pulled off this stateside success story. Speaking of the big bands who had flopped in America, he said: 'I think with most of these bands, you end up with a sound that sounds somewhere between England and America – which means you fall smack down in the middle of the ocean. You don't appeal to either.' The vehicle that drove the success was, without a doubt, online social networking. Thanks to Twitter, Facebook and Tumblr, the band was already being marketed in the States by the most enthusiastic team possible: the fans themselves. Justin Bieber's success, which was originally largely down to YouTube and Twitter, had taught everyone a lesson: teenage acts can bypass the old-fashioned promotional routes. As such, Cowell could afford to be optimistic. He noticed, as he launched *The X Factor USA* in 2011, that already teenage girls there were taking an interest in the band. They kept asking him when he would bring One Direction to America.

Therefore, he allowed this frenzy to build organically. 'Normally we hassle the American labels when we think something is going to work,' he told *Rolling Stone*. 'This time we said, "Let's just wait for the phone to ring and see who phones first". I wanted them to find out about the group first in a more buzzy way rather than us forcing the band on them.'

While Cowell believes that the impact of social networking on the industry is 'great news' and that 'for the music business, social networking is brilliant', he is at pains to emphasize that an act needs an inherent charm and spark in order to make a success of this very modern method of marketing. 'The band has to make it happen by themselves,' he said. 'I think that's what One Direction did. We worked as a partnership, but without their input and the way they spoke to the fans and the kind of people they are, it wouldn't have happened in the way that it's happening now.'

One of Cowell's key employees agrees. 'Sometimes you feel the song's the star, but it's not like that here – it's the act,' Sonny Takhar, managing director of Syco, told the *Guardian*.

'It's a real moment,' added Takhar. 'Social media has become the new radio, it's never broken an act globally like this before.' How sustainable social media is in this sense remains to be seen. For instance, while Lily Allen and Arctic Monkeys used the MySpace network to great effect in launching their careers, the tsunami of mediocre acts that then flooded MySpace with their own material quickly devalued the forum. As Cowell himself admits, 'there's tons of groups out there. It doesn't happen to everyone.'

In addition to the factors outlined by Cowell, one should consider that the American market had a yawning gap for a new boy band. The likes of the New Kids on the Block, the Backstreet Boys and 'N Sync had never been truly replaced there. Even The Jonas Brothers, who in any case inhabited a slightly different part of the market, had long since peaked. One Direction, and their fellow British boy band The Wanted, came along at just the right time. One Direction's stateside success can be explained by a potent combination of charm and timing: they arrived as a new method of marketing was in its ascendancy and when the market itself was craving an act such as theirs. Some guys get all the luck.

However, not everything went their way in America. Soon after they arrived, news broke that a US band, also called One Direction, were planning to sue over the use of their name by the British band. The US band's lawyer, Peter Ross, claimed to the *Hollywood Reporter* that the band and their management had been made aware for a while of the name-clash issue. 'Rather than change their name or do anything to create confusion or avoid damage to our goodwill, they chose to press ahead and come on their tour,' Ross said. 'We've been in negotiations for a month to find a resolution. In our view, the negotiations weren't turning out to be very productive.'

Even as this tangle continued, the band had plenty to console themselves with. Their popularity did not diminish at all as a result of the dispute. Indeed, if anything it solidified the support of the fans for the British band. It gave everyone something to unite against. On Twitter and other social networking websites the almost unanimous response to the battle was one of support for the British band. Asked on

Australian television if they would be changing their name, Harry and Zayn both said 'no'. Zayn then added: 'We don't know [what will happen] but we're not changing our name.'

Alongside this surge of love and support was the fact that the five lads were making serious money from their success. There has sometimes been a perception that even those who build a successful career from *The X Factor* never make any money. Instead, goes the belief, the managers of said career cream off all the money, leaving mere peanuts for the artists themselves, who are locked into contracts that are cleverly designed to throw them only scraps. However, the experience of acts as diverse as Leona Lewis and Jedward suggests otherwise. Both are authoritatively perceived to have made a great deal of money since their *X Factor* experiences.

In the case of One Direction, reports claimed that as of April 2012 each member had already made over £1 million. 'Simon Cowell wants them to know what they deserve. They have been a massive success, what they have achieved is phenomenal. Simon thinks they are the hardest-working people in pop at the moment,' a source told the *People*. In the same month, some statistics emerged to backup that figure. For instance, 'What Makes You Beautiful' went platinum in the US after selling 1,129,852 units in the first few months after its release. This was quite remarkable by any standards. Established British bands would struggle to do so well in America. For a band to do that well with their debut was almost unparalleled.

Meanwhile, they were touring Australia and New Zealand. What an experience all this travelling was for the boys, not least Zayn, who had never been abroad until he took part in *The X Factor*. When they appeared on Australian television, hundreds of fans flocked to stand outside the studio and scream their love for the band. 'This is mental, it's absolutely incredible and we can't believe it,' said Liam when he and his band-mates saw the scenes. The hysteria was shocking and the police had to work hard to maintain order. One fan said she would be willing to be shot by a stun gun to get close to her heartthrobs. 'I'll do anything to see them, I'd even get tasered for this,' she said. The band made such an impact Down Under that when tickets for their eighteen shows to be held there in September 2013 went on sale, all 190,000 were instantly snapped-up. Country by country, One Direction was conquering the world.

10 THE PRICE OF FAME

During an interview in America, Liam had opened up about the price that comes with fame – especially fame acquired at high speed. 'It's all happening so fast, it's hard to take it all in,' he said. 'Sometimes it's only when I'm on my own, that I think about everything and sometimes I think I would quite like to just go home. There's a part of me that occasionally wants to go back to Wolverhampton and just chill out, play the field, be normal again. It's a Catch 22 situation, I guess.' Given the media training each band member had undergone, this was a surprisingly candid moment from Liam. His words reflected each band members' awareness that the relentless workload, insatiable scrutiny and undoubted pressure that they faced as celebrities could sometimes seem too much to take. Liam, who dates dancer Danielle Peazer, was under no illusion that amid the scrutiny the band faced came almost excruciating attention on their love lives. It was never going to be otherwise, particularly for a band whose appeal was to a large extent based on how they look.

It had been the same ever since the band was first formed. Even while their *X Factor* series was still ongoing, Zayn was rumoured to be dating Geneva Lane, a member of the girl band Belle Amie. The speculation reached fever pitch when he was spotted kissing her backstage during the final weekend of the series. He was then seen holding hands with Lane, who is three years his senior, as they left the studios. As far as the press was concerned these photographs proved the rumours to be true. Zayn, though, had news for them. He wrote on Twitter: 'Hey fans, just thought I'd let u guys know don't believe the hype we're just friends and that was a friendly kiss.'

The picture was further muddled by the fact that Lane had earlier, seemingly, confirmed on Twitter that there was a relationship between her and Zayn. 'We have a thing,' she had said during a Twitter exchange with a friend. Her connection with Zayn, whatever the extent and nature of it, meant she was targeted by fans who thought she might be a useful 'in' for them with the band. She was bombarded with requests to pass messages to the band, including requests that she set up a coveted 'follow' on Twitter. 'You know, I find it a bit disrespectful that some people on here consider me to be a personal assistant to 1D,' she wrote.

Lane was not the only *X Factor* finalist Zayn has been linked with. He was also reported to have dated runner-up Rebecca Ferguson – and this time the rumours were confirmed. 'I'm in love and it's a wonderful feeling', said Ferguson during an interview with *Reveal* magazine. 'I've never felt like this before. It took a while before we looked at each other in a different light. There was no one particular moment, it just evolved over time. But he made all the running.' Several reports had stated that it was Zayn who had been the driving force between the couple getting together. One described him as 'very persuasive' when it came to women.

However, the most notorious relationship

involving a member of One Direction was, of course, Harry's relationship with *Xtra Factor* host Caroline Flack. This proved to be a sensational story from the start: the teenage *X Factor* contestant in a dalliance with a thirty-something presenter. He posted a sign that read: 'To Flackster! Never too old ... Let's make it happen!! Lots of love, Harry S.' Reports suggested that they did indeed quickly make it happen: the fling started after he had described her as 'gorgeous' and was then seen smooching with her at an after-show party. Flack soon discovered that any woman – particularly an older one – who was linked with a member of the band, would soon face enormous abuse on the internet. For her, this included being bombarded with death threats every time the media stitched together any details about the romance.

Rebecca Ferguson had already complained about 'abuse' from 'twelve year olds' during her relationship with Zayn. It seemed that Flack faced an even more fierce backlash, including on Twitter. After feeling sickened by the flood of threats and abuse she was facing, she sent a message out in response. 'Hi one direction fans! To clarify. I'm close friends with harry ... He's one of the nicest people I know ... I don't deserve death threats :) x.' Reports suggested that Harry's mum was unimpressed, too, and wanted Flack to 'keep your hands off my son!'

Given the hectic demands of both parties' careers and the enormous scrutiny they faced as a couple, it was less than shocking when it was revealed that they had split. Harry was said to be the one who called time on the relationship, but, sensitive to the possible damage that being perceived as a 'dumper' might cause to his image, he made a rare statement on Twitter: 'Please know I didn't "dump" Caroline. This was a mutual decision. She is one of the kindest, sweetest people I know. Please respect that.'

When things had calmed down, Flack finally spoke with more candour about what they had been through. Even then, though, she left much to the imagination. 'Harry is adorable, he is a nice person,' she told the *Mail on Sunday*. She said that, despite the split, they remained on good terms. 'First and foremost we are friends. We got very close for a time but that's between me and Harry. What happened is between me and him and then we decided it was best to just be friends.'

Still, the relationship had become one of the biggest celebrity sagas of recent years and has created a variety of responses. Flack was simultaneously lauded for bagging a hot young man and slammed for being little better than a cradle-snatcher, while Harry faced similar contrary responses. He was soon handed the reputation of a young man who is a passionate admirer of the older lady. He did little to dispel this perception when he subsequently hinted he had a thing for thirty-something socialite Kim Kardashian. During an interview in America he held up a poster of the curvy celebrity, attached to it was a Post-it note on which he had scribbled: 'Call me ... Maybe?' Then, during a television interview, Zayn teased Harry about his perceived penchant. 'He likes an older woman,' said Zayn, much to Harry's discomfort. 'What's your rule? Anyone younger than ...' It was then that Harry stepped in to stop Zayn going any further. His humour on the issue is wearing thin.

Sadly, the abiding memory from any

encounter a member of One Direction had with a member of the fairer sex was the hassle that came with it for both parties, particularly the female. So intense was the fans' devotion to the band that a vocal minority of them were willing and – thanks to the online age – able to make life hell for any girl who got close to the band. Liam's girlfriend Danielle had received some unpleasant messages herself. Even Hannah Walker, a pretty blonde who was dating Louis long before he became famous, was ruthlessly targeted on Twitter.

This is a perpetually smouldering issue but occasionally it ignites into something fiercer. For instance, in April 2012, twenty-year-old Anna Crotti said she had been 'bullied' online into cancelling a date with Zayn. She had met him during the band's stay in Australia. 'A security guard came up to me. I thought I was in trouble but he said, "The lads want your number",' she told MTV. 'I got a text later saying hello. I asked who it was and it was Zayn.' Word soon got out that she was speaking with Zayn, and that was when the trouble started.

'By the end of the day, it got a bit too scary,'

she said. 'Random girls were abusing me on Facebook. Girls were calling the radio station and giving me s**t. Mothers even called me in tears, demanding to know if I knew where One Direction were because their daughters wanted to meet them. I didn't even want to walk home. It was so intense. I messaged Zayn and said, "Maybe it's not a good idea we meet up". It was just a bit too full on.'

During the same trip, renewed speculation was surrounding Harry's love life. While they were in New Zealand, he reportedly began dating American model Emma Ostilly. He was said to have taken her on a date and smooched on her doorstep. 'They really seemed to have a connection and only had eyes for each other', an onlooker was quoted as saying. The suspiciously familiar vocabulary – used in endless quotes from unnamed 'sources' – brought the veracity of this into question. After Harry explained that she was 'just a friend', Liam backed up his band mate, saying: 'She's not his girlfriend either'. This was not enough to save her from some fans' venom. She deleted her Twitter account after tiring of the hassle.

The band became increasingly frustrated when they saw what girls they were linked to had to endure. They were in a bizarre position: millions of girls around the world were desperate to fling themselves at them, yet the flipside of that fact made them strangely difficult young men to date. The band could have been forgiven if they were left wondering whether the 'fans' who bombarded their partners with online abuse were really worthy to be described as 'fans' at all. Later in April, Louis showed that his patience was wearing ever thinner when he confronted his fans on Twitter. He discovered that, under the hashtag 'Louannah' – a nickname used during his relationship with Hannah Walker – fans had been Tweeting his then-girlfriend Eleanor Calder with photographs of him with Walker. He was furious and took to Twitter to make his feelings known. In an uncharacteristic outburst, he wrote: 'Truth of the matter is its actually not funny in the slightest. I'm reading through some horrible tweets very p*ssed off!' He also sent a message directly to Calder, reassuring her of his feelings: 'Love YOU! xxxx' and then added: 'I couldn't be happier right now, so let it be :) Thank youuuuu x.' He knew his fans would see this message, so it was partially addressed to them, too.

Meanwhile Hannah Walker, a primary school teaching assistant who had taken a step back from the limelight since her split with Louis, was dragged back into the fray. She told the *Daily Mail* she was embarrassed by the fuss and that she had taken the trouble to contact Eleanor Calder to tell her it had nothing to do with her. As for her famous ex-boyfriend, she said: 'When I look at him on the television now I know him as two different people – one is the boy from Doncaster, and the other is Louis from One Direction.' She just wanted Louis to be happy and it is safe to say that the majority of One Direction fans feel exactly the same way.

It is worth reflecting on the experience of other boy bands to understand how One Direction stand out in regard to their relationships with women. In days gone by, boy band members were often banned by their management from having girlfriends, or at least publicly admitting as much. Take That, for instance, were ordered not to have girlfriends by their management team as it was feared that they would lose appeal to their fans if they were not perceived as being 'available' romantically. For One Direction, a decision was taken early on that a different approach would be taken. They would be allowed to have girlfriends and to be open about this. At one early meeting with their management the boys were even encouraged to date slightly older women, as it was felt the 'fall out' following any split would be less damaging that way.

The different approach to One Direction's image informs the whole package. 'We're trying to do something different from what people would think is the typical kind of boy band,' Niall told Canada's *National Post*. 'We're trying to do different kinds of music and we're just trying to be ourselves, not squeaky clean.' In time, this frenzy that surrounds the girls that any band member is dating may calm; as the real fans, who only wish the boys well, make their voices heard above the din, life will improve for all concerned.

Lest we forget, the One Direction fans are

a lovely and loving clan. They have frequently used Twitter to create supportive and kind trends. The band members' frustration over the girlfriend issue was put into perspective by the news that Zayn's aunt had died in February 2012. This happened while the band was in America. A flight was swiftly booked so Zayn could rush home to be with his family. The news was announced by Harry on Twitter: 'Zayn has suffered a loss in his family & has had to go home for a few days so won't be at our next shows in the US,' wrote Harry. 'Our thoughts are with him and his family at this sad time.'

The fans were upset to think of their hero suffering – particularly after his grandfather's death during the *X Factor* live shows. They started a hash-tag tribute for Zayn and his family, getting the '#StayStrongZayn' to trend on the social network. The first interaction Zayn himself made following his bereavement was to 're-tweet' a message from another user. It read: 'God has no Phone, but I talk to him. He has no Facebook, but he is still my friend. He does not have a twitter, but I still follow him. (sic)' That story reflects the real fans of

One Direction, who will stick with the band in the future. Having supported them from the very beginning, the fans know that they had – and still have – a part to play in this remarkable story.

11 LIVING WHILE THEY'RE YOUNG

The Mayans prophesied that the world would end in 2012. To the relief of many, the world did not end – but planet pop did submit to the rule of One Direction. Their debut album continued to sell strongly, ultimately reaching number one in more than sixteen countries: its successor would hit the top spot in more than twice as many territories.

The fantastic five's popularity and influence soared throughout the year, and with it, their profits: by June, their business empire, which stretched across the globe, was worth $50bn. The band became almost a mini industry in its own right: the immediate team who were specifically employed to look after One Direction – including managers, stylists and producers – was ninety-strong. With their success in the all-important American market growing apace, it was expected that their profits would only continue to rise in the years ahead, with their record label confidently predicting they would double their income in 2013.

It was a breathless and brilliant year. Musically, its peak came in November when the band's second album was released. The shrewdly titled *Take Me Home* had, throughout its production, been seen as a fresh and valued opportunity to inject the band's music with a sense of their own individuality and appeal. 'It's important to get their personalities on the music', songwriter Richard Falk told the *Independent*. The band was not short of ideas on how to achieve this. Harry spoke for all five when he outlined the manifesto for the album: 'a lot less little synth sounds, more guitars and drums'. The result was a long player that confounded expectation.

The album opens with the attention-grabbing guitar riff that heralds their hit 'Live While We're Young'. The song is familiar territory, similar in structure, tone and overall theme to 'What Makes You Beautiful'. However the album also had several surprises up its sleeves. Track two,

'Kiss You', is their most energetic romp to date – a breathless and catchy three minutes of pop. For as long as it appears on the set-list of One Direction's live shows the five boys will have to keep fit in order to perform its fast, potentially tongue-tying lyrics. The album's third song is its biggest revelation. Co-written by Ed Sheeran and Fiona Bevan, 'Little Things' is like nothing the band had recorded before; it is a gentle acoustic ballad with lyrics that express emotional depths the band had never previously hinted at. Niall noticed how the success of 'Little Things' saw their fan-base widen both in number and demographic variety. 'It's broadening the audience for sure,' he told Billboard. 'I get a lot of dudes, a lot of moms and dads coming up and saying they love it.' (Sheeran, who is close friends with the band, also wrote another of the album's tracks – the less memorable 'Over Again'.)

'Last First Kiss' is another mature ballad, though of a heavier weight than 'Little Things'. Another track, 'Change My Mind' would, both musically and lyrically, have been deemed too mature for their debut album. Yet it sits comfortably in *Take Me Home*, as does 'Back For You', in which the innocent boys of yesteryear hint at more adult and raunchy intentions with the ever-present female characters of their music. It is safe to say, judging by the unflinching suggestions that thousands of fans 'tweet' to the boys each day, that few of their fans were to be offended by the song, which Louis has described as feeling, 'quite band-y'.

Elsewhere, while the opening to 'Live While We're Young' had earned on-the-money comparisons with British punk band The Clash, in 'Rock Me' it is another 1970s band that comes to mind: the clapping beat being reminiscent of Queen. For the second album running, a track written by McFly is included, in the shape of 'I Would'. However the inclusion of the song caused some controversy when, during an interview with the *Metro* newspaper, McFly's Danny Jones suggested they had palmed One Direction off with inferior material. The story created quite a storm and Jones's band mate Tom Fletcher was quick to issue a denial, stating it was 'obviously completely false' and that Jones had only been joking.

As for the tracks written by the band members themselves, One Direction found that their most productive sessions were not as a five. 'It was actually usually groups of three,' said Liam. 'It's nice to have two people around. When you have more than two people working together it gets a bit unfocused as an idea.'

These song-writing sessions, and those of the band's talented creative contacts, had produced a fine set of pop tunes that built into a memorable and well-received album. The *Independent* declared *Take Me Home* to be: 'sing-into-your-hairbrush, life-enhancing pop,' which 'has "OMG!!!!" written all over it'. Over the water, the *Boston Globe* deemed it: 'uniformly sleek and upbeat', while *Rolling Stone* magazine preferred the heavier tracks to the lighter efforts, ruling that *Take Me Home*: 'rivals the best of Backstreet and 'N Sync when the material pumps'.

Commercially, there was no such equivocation: the album was a solid smash hit. It reached number one in a staggering thrity-five countries, including the UK, USA, Canada and Australia. Those cynics who had insisted One Direction would be a 'one-hit wonder' were forced to revise their sour verdicts: incredibly, the already-huge boy band was actually growing in popularity.

Louis, Liam, Niall, Zayn and Harry had also been busy on the live circuit throughout 2012, putting in a string of polished performances that built on their previous shows. As well as belting out their own material, they continued to perform cover versions of other artists' music, including the Wheatus hit 'Teenage Dirtbag'. It was Louis who first suggested they include the punk-pop classic in their live repertoire. Initially, his suggestion was not universally welcomed. 'The minute he said it everyone was like, "yeah let's do it!" except for me,' admitted Zayn during a chat with *Billboard*. 'The boys were laughing. It grew on me, though.'

Throughout 2012, their live shows garnered praise from even the hardest to please of media critics. Repeatedly, the reviewers expressed pleasant surprise at the level of vocal ability and overall showmanship. They were not just a bunch of pretty faces after all, journalists reported. As *Rolling Stone* commented on a live performance: 'There was no need to worry about a backing track or a bum note, a pleasant realization at a pop show.'

The lack of dancing in the performance also prompted interest. Boy bands of the 1990s had been as much about closely choreographed dancing as they had vocals. With One Direction, this is not the case. 'We don't dance because we can't dance,' Louis told *Billboard*. 'Our shows, production-wise, are always quite minimal.'

Another positive oddity of the band is that their vocal talents are essentially equal: in previous boy bands there has traditionally been one particularly strong member (Bobby Brown, Justin Timberlake, Michael Jackson, etc.) Several commentators identified Niall as the most natural overall live performer. He told *Vogue* why he so enjoys touring. 'I love it,' he said. 'I love the screaming. They love it, too: they've all got their tickets and they've been waiting a year or so to see you, so you've got to give it your best.' Both band and audience determined to have the night of their lives: no wonder tickets to their shows are in such demand.

As well as concerts, One Direction performed

on television shows, at award ceremonies and at other special events, including a memorable appearance at the 2012 Olympic closing ceremony. For Harry, their evening at the Olympic village was his personal highlight of the year. 'For me the Olympics literally can't be topped,' he said. 'Just the feeling of being in that room, all our families were there. The whole feeling was just unbelievable.'

He also enjoyed their appearance at the MTV Video Music Awards (VMAs), during which the band were able to show the cream of the music industry just how accomplished they are as performers.

The highlight of the year for their American fans came at New York's landmark venue, Madison Square Garden. Only the very elite members of the world of pop have performed at this iconic stadium. For each member of the band, particularly the America-crazy Liam, this was a special moment. As they crouched backstage, waiting to be propelled in front of the 20,000-strong audience, they could hardly believe they were playing there. The fact they had sold out the venue within sixty seconds of the tickets going on sale only swelled their pride – and their pre-show anxiety.

Louis had been nervous that their rehearsals for the show might not have been sufficiently thorough. It all went swimmingly, though, and throughout the pulsating performance the band remarked on their excitement. 'I'm overwhelmed,' Zayn told the screaming fans. 'I'm from a small town in Bradford. Things like this don't happen to people like me.' Niall added: 'This is the best night of our lives. You guys have travelled from all around the world and we cannot believe what has happened here tonight.' Ed Sheeran joined them on-stage for their rendition of 'Little Things', and by the time they crowned the encore with their debut hit 'What Makes You Beautiful', they had New York in the palms of their hands. Later, they partied the night away at the Hudson Hotel.

Then it was back to work, for the One Direction machine is a beast that allows no resting on laurels. In November 2012, they announced plans to release their own big-screen movie. Following the example of Justin Bieber's enormously successful movie *Never Say*

Never, they decided it would be filmed in 3D. It will be directed by Morgan Spurlock, perhaps best known for his work on the documentary *Supersize Me*. The director described the task in suitably awed tones, dubbing it an 'epic undertaking'.

Simon Cowell, meanwhile, said the film is for the fans, to honour how they 'have made history around the world'. Niall promised MTV that the film would give a chance for the fans to get more intimate with the boys. He said the intention was to 'get our personalities across' so their fans can 'get to know us deeper'. Niall was handed a video camera, so he could record some raw footage to add to the mix. Harry feels the film will be a great personal document, which will be of interest for future generations of the Styles family. 'Just to have the ability to be able to kind of look back at that when we're older and to have your children see it will be amazing,' he said. When the film is released in August 2013 it is bound to provoke a stampede of fans.

Meanwhile, the band continued its own determined march. *Billboard* magazine named

One Direction its Top New Artist of 2012. 'It's absolutely amazing to have that kind of recognition in America,' said Louis in response to the honour. The American success has hugely boosted their overall commercial performance: as of the autumn of 2012, the band had sold over fifteen million records worldwide – a phenomenal number, particularly in an era in which overall record sales have dipped. All of this success has naturally brought increased personal riches to the band members. In October they reached *Heat* magazine's rich list of young stars, thanks to their estimated collective personal fortunes of £26.33m.

Yet there are always costs to be met: just as they have amassed riches, so have the band been forced to sacrifice their privacy. Each of the band members has had to face enormous intrusion into their personal lives. When Liam split with girlfriend Danielle Peazer, the story became a media sensation – indeed discussion of the split was so intense on social networks that websites such as Twitter strained under the weight of commentary from fans. Likewise, Louis, Zayn and Harry have also faced relentless attention from snappers and scribes, eager to land lucrative exclusives. Even Niall, who has remained single, has faced probing speculation over his personal life. In the world of pop, only Justin Bieber faces more aggressive press attention. In January 2013, the danger of such pressure to all parties became clear when a paparazzo was killed in a car crash while chasing a photograph of Bieber. Everyone in the industry felt shaken.

However it is Harry's personal life that has attracted the most attention. Following his rumoured romance with Caroline Flack, his romantic activities have become nothing short of a fascination. Media portrayals of Harry as a rampaging lothario are exaggerated, but now that the media has awarded him the reputation of a 'player', it will be disinclined to relieve him of it. When he began to date the singer Taylor Swift, they were quickly installed as pop's golden couple. They were spotted kissing after Swift's New Year's concert in New York and they then holidayed together in the Caribbean. Unconfirmed reports suggested that Harry had told Swift he 'loved' her, and that her father had warned young Harry to take the relationship seriously and not break his daughter's heart. While some One Direction fans were pleased to see their hero seemingly settled in a relationship, many were furious with Swift and vented their feelings on social networks.

While the band members are aware that such intensity comes with the territory of the fame they have worked so hard to acquire, they can justifiably feel aggrieved at the extent to which their every move provokes such forceful emotions.

Liam wrestled back an element of anonymity when he had his much-loved locks shaved off, leaving him with a closely cropped look. It was a moment of rebellion from the heartthrob. 'At the start, the management said I wasn't allowed to change my hair,' he told *Vogue*. 'But then I did it anyway, so they kind of let that one go.' Suddenly, he was able to walk around the streets of Britain and America without being recognized. One day, he donned a decoy outfit – he was, he said, 'dressed as a big chav – Adidas trainers, jogging bottoms' – and walked around revelling in his newfound anonymity. Naturally, as his new hairstyle became recognizable, his period of relative personal serenity passed. He had so enjoyed it.

In truth, sometimes the band is complicit in stoking the media fire. In November 2012, members of One Direction engaged in a Twitter spat with members of rival boy band The Wanted. It was a fulsome and adult exchange that hinted at a member of One Direction using marijuana – and gave the band's handlers a challenging public relations problem. While the band has never been presented as angelic or whiter-than-white, all concerned with One Direction's image are conscious of how important that image is – especially if it gives a less than ideal message to the band's youngest fans. It also increases the pressure on the band from the media, as photographers sense a chance for a new 'money shot'. However, the band has denied that any of its members has ever touched drugs, and asked about drugs during a press conference in Madrid, Louis said: 'we don't need any of that [drug use]. We'll just stick to the Pepsi!'

The band's families have also suffered under the strain of their ascendancy. While their relatives are enormously proud of the success of the five members, they are upset by some of the media intrusion and online abuse that the boys face, especially when it spills over into family life. They also miss the boys while they are away, busy conquering the globe.

Time with their families has been at a premium since the band's formation. A three-day break during 2012 was one of their lengthiest rests to date. The boys so looked forward to the seventy-two hours of downtime, with Niall beside himself with excitement at being able to spend a few days 'hanging out at home and going to the pub with my old mates'. Zayn's mother, Tricia, said: 'When he leaves home I cry at the gate and he says: "Mum! I'm not going to war!"' Conjuring a heart-breaking image, she added: 'A driver comes for him and I have to stand there and wave back.'

Such departures will continue for the foreseeable future as One Direction remain the toast of pop. At the time of writing, the band has not forgotten where they came from. Zayn's name-checking of Bradford during their Madison Square Garden concert indicated this. Liam, meanwhile, made a physical promise to remain grounded when he tattooed, 'Everything I Ever Wanted, But Nothing I'll Ever Need' on his arm. For him, this was a permanent reminder that while his wildest pop dreams were being realized, the important things in his life remain the love of his family and friends.

Remarkably, as recently as 2010 these had been five unknown boys whose social diaries were just like those of any ordinary British teenager. Yet, as 2012 eased into 2013, their future schedule was positively glittering, including a world tour of over 100 dates, further recording sessions, appearances on red carpets, and more. So here's to the future of One Direction and their continuing global pillage.

Robbie Williams compared the band to the biggest UK pop act of recent decades. 'They're quite a power in the way the Spice Girls were,' he told *The Sun*. 'The Spice Girls took over the world and won and I think the One Direction boys have a similar chemistry.' How far the band had come since they had nervously performed with Williams during the *X Factor* live shows.

Simon Cowell, their *X Factor* mentor, remains enormously proud of them. They have become his trump calling card in America and he is keenly focused on ensuring their continued success. Niall says they are still in regular contact with Cowell. 'Luckily enough we've never had to disagree,' he said of their relationship with the notoriously outspoken judge.

Having noted the creative progressions in *Take Me Home*, it will be fascinating to see how the band's musical output develops. One Direction have admitted that, to a large extent, their personal musical tastes differ from the majority of the music they have released on their first two albums. They are fans of a wide range of genres – from folk and country to punk-pop, indie and hip hop. Their tour bus rocks to the sounds of acts such as The Fray, The Lumineers, Elvis Perkins, Passenger, Lady Antebellum, Jay Z and Kanye West. If these artists begin to influence One Direction's output, the band will become increasingly attached to their music, which can only prolong their career. 'We want to gradually get more and more "live" sounding,' Harry told *Vogue*.

It is essential that the ideas, wishes and thoughts of the band members themselves are always at the centre of their development. The lads do not wish to be pop puppets and neither would their fans stand for that. These are five lads with a real creative spark. They are also five decent and kind young men who deserve to be respected. Simon Cowell was once asked how he would make sure that the band sustain their success, rather than fizzing quickly out of favour in the ever-fickle pop industry. His philosophy was simple: 'Be sensible and treat them as human beings, genuinely. That's the most important thing.'

INDEX

(1D in subentries refers to One Direction)

INDEX

INDEX

BIBLIOGRAPHY

Birth Order, Linda Blair, Piatkus Books, 2011

One Direction A-Z, Sarah Oliver, John Blake Publishing, 2011

One Direction: Dare to Dream: Life as One Direction, One Direction, HarperCollins, 2011

1D: Forever Young, One Direction, HarperCollins, 2011

Simon Cowell: The Unauthorized Biography, Chas Newkey-Burden, Michael O'Mara Books, 2009

The X Factor: Access All Areas, Jordan Paramor, Headline, 2007

PICTURE CREDITS